Living Magic

Living
Magic

THE REALITIES UNDERLYING THE PSYCHICAL PRACTICES

AND BELIEFS OF AUSTRALIAN ABORIGINES

by Ronald Rose

RAND McNALLY & COMPANY

New York · Chicago · San Francisco

FOREWORD

It is rarely that one finds a book of scientific exploration interestingly written. The careful scholarly author tries to evaluate as he writes and all too often loses his readers' interest by his tedious academic qualification. Ronald Rose, however, will take his readers with him every fascinating step of the way, even through his final experimental chapter.

The experiments which he and his wife, Lyndon, have conducted to test the psi ("psychic") capacities of the Australian Aborigines have been outstanding pioneer studies. The fact that there has been so little of this kind of research gives some indication of the difficulty of the task. Indeed the Roses must have shown a high order of skill in so adapting their "white man's tests" to the aborigines that the delicate abilities being tested were not entirely inhibited. The results obtained compare favorably with the range of scores obtained with Caucasians in Europe and America.

But just as I venture to suggest the readers of this book will, in their way, see to it that this is not the last its author will write, so I trust those who appreciate the experimental work behind it will see to it that the experimental studies too are followed up. Because I think they will be, I will make one prediction: It will surprise me greatly indeed if further efforts in adapting the test of psychokinesis to the culture of the aborigines did not eventually yield the same positive results on that aspect of psi capacity that the Roses obtained in their E.S.P. tests with them. That is just one of the many challenges this volume plants in our minds.

J. B. RHINE, *Director*
Parapsychology Laboratory
Duke University

Acknowledgments

For permission to reprint material on the pages given below, from the published sources indicated, the author and his publisher gratefully extend their thanks to the following publishers:

Angus & Robertson, Ltd., Sydney, Australia, for the quotation on pages 146–47, from *The Australian Aborigines,* by A. P. Elkin.

The Australasian Publishing Company, Sydney, Australia, for the quotation on page 19, from *Aboriginal Men of High Degree,* by A. P. Elkin.

Constable & Co., Ltd., London, England, for the quotations on pages 121 and 182–83, from *The Euahlayi Tribe,* by K. Langloh Parker.

Macmillan & Co., Ltd., London, England, for the quotation on pages 74–75 and 163–64, from *The Native Tribes of South-East Australia,* by A. W. Howitt.

The publishers of the journal *Oceania,* Sydney, Australia, for the quotation on page 67, from an article, "Wuradjeri Magic," by R. M. Berndt.

Routledge & Kegan Paul Ltd., London, England, for the quotation on page 186, from *Aboriginal Woman,* by Phyllis M. Kaberry.

CONTENTS

In the fully tribal state aborigines wear no clothes.
They build only the most primitive, temporary dwellings.
They have only stone or wooden implements.
They harvest no crops, living by hunting
and gathering roots and berries.

The mythical rainbow snake, believed source of aboriginal
doctors' magic, portrayed in a rock drawing by Yungitcha.

Much of the route traversed between Hermannsburg and Areyonga
comprised rough, red boulders such as these, that tore shoes to shreds
in half a day's travel. It was country never before seen by whites.

Clumps of spinifex mottle the red sand
at the base of the Krichauff Range.

Tribal natives in Central Australia
often wear bones through
their pierced septums.
Here Tjalkalieri demonstrates
the fashion. This bone
after appropriate
ceremony
can be used to kill
a man by "pointing."

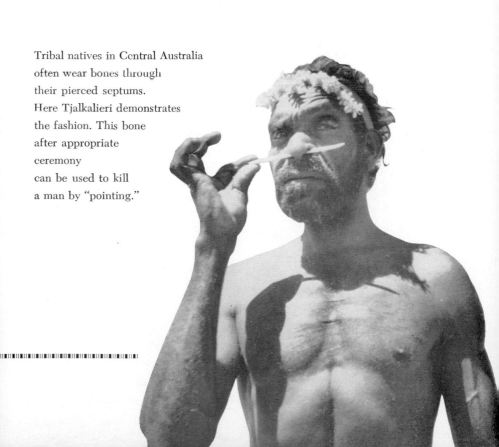

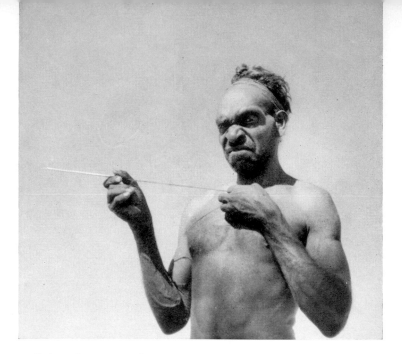

Tjalkalieri demonstrates bone pointing.
The bone has a human hair cord attachment.
He would not point the bone directly at me for a photograph,
fearing its deadly power would harm me.

Winjin shows the use of the spear thrower,
or *woomera,* which acts as an extension of the arm.
Natives, with this weapon, will stalk kangaroos for miles.

Yungitcha,
a Pitjendadjara,
examines
a love-magic token.
Natives believe that,
when such an object
is swung on
a human hair cord,
the girl whom
the young man desires
responds to the noise,
and comes to him,
often traveling
great distances.

A sacred *churinga* of the Aranda Tribe,
marked with secret totemic designs.

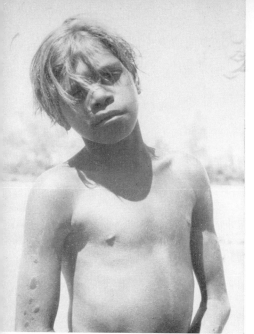

Kinchika's arms show
tribal markings burnt
into his flesh
as part of his initiation.

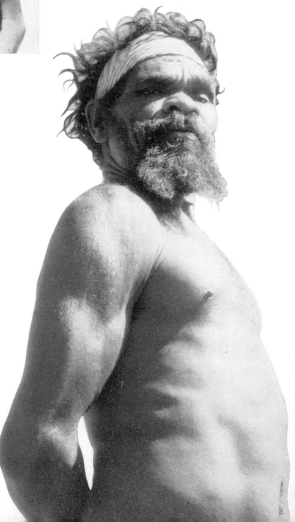

Winjin was a
fine physical specimen,
a tribal doctor
or clever-man of
the Pitjendadjara tribe
in Areyonga Valley.

Maleiaba, an Ayers Rock native.
He is carrying a wooden barbed spear. The barb is held
firmly with kangaroo sinews which become taut as they dry.

Kurdaitcha shoes,
worn by *kurdaitcha*
killing parties,
resemble bird nests.
They are made from feathers,
twigs, and human blood.
The wearers must
dislocate a toe
before the shoes
may be worn.

Tjalkalieri displays
an ancient stone
tribal *churinga,*
a sacred relic of
the Pitjendadjara.
A human hair cord
is threaded through
a hole in the *churinga.*

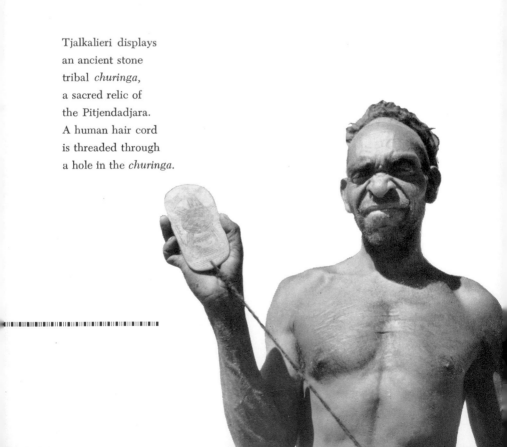

INTRODUCTION

Although a good deal of the matter this book describes comes, or should come, within the province of the anthropologist, this is not an anthropological account. It is essentially the story of how parapsychological tests were applied to Australian aborigines in an attempt to determine the fact or fancy underlying their magic. This was the first occasion that such tests were administered with primitive subjects anywhere.

Parapsychology is a comparatively new experimental science employing laboratory-type tests and depending on statistical interpretation. Its field of investigation covers extrasensory perception and psychokinesis. These are scientific terms covering mental phenomena commonly described as telepathic or clairvoyant in the first instance and mind-over-matter in the second.

Let it be said right from the outset that my wife and I found a great deal of evidence for the existence of extrasensory perception (or telepathy) among aborigines, thus tending to substantiate some of the claims of their magic—but not all of them, of course. We found no conclusive evidence for mind-over-matter phenomena. On the other hand we did find evidence of the skillful use of hypnotism; and we found imposture and fraud, superstition and delusion, distortion, exaggeration, and sheer fancy.

The problem was to sift the wheat from the chaff. Our tools were the sets of tests and questionnaires described.

(See Appendixes A and B.) Associated with the major problem were other, human, problems, such as gaining the confidence of the aborigines and winning their co-operation. It was only after nearly six years of close association with one group of natives, for example, that I was able to get any concrete information on their magic-cord phenomena. Information of any value on aboriginal magic cannot be obtained in brief visits to camps when informants are hurried and harried. Neither can the tests, which depend so vitally on the rapport between experimenters and subjects, be properly conducted in such circumstances.

Research into aspects of the personality, whether on an individual or a social level, has its own special rewards, however. It is always a co-operative affair.

One requires subjects. My wife and I had the generous assistance of aboriginal subjects and informants ranging from the almost fully tribal Pitjendadjara, the remnants of the Aranda and other Central Australian tribes, to detribalized natives stemming principally from the Bundulung and Gidabul groups on the east coast. Some of them were more than merely subjects—they became guides, interpreters, and friends.

Numbers of authorities on aboriginal culture, principally Professor A. P. Elkin, and Catherine and Ronald Berndt, of the University of Sydney, gave generously of their advice and assistance.

Government authorities gave their approval for us to enter areas forbidden to the tourist. These authorities included the Native Affairs Department of the Northern Territory and the Aborigines Welfare Board of New South Wales. Officers of these departments, such as Mr. and Mrs. J. B. Stratton, manager and matron of Woodenbong Aboriginal Settlement, went far beyond the call of official duty in extending their hospitality to us and accommodating us in their home during the testing programs.

Lutheran missionaries at Hermannsburg and Areyonga (the pastors F. W. Albrecht and V. Koschade) helped us with the natives, with accommodations, and in organizing our camel teams.

From America came aid in the way of technical advice on parapsychological and statistical matters from Dr. J. B. Rhine and Dr. J. B. Pratt of Duke University, North Carolina, and generous grants from the Parapsychology Foundation, Inc., New York, through its president, Mrs. Eileen Garrett, to enable us to complete the work on the east coast.

Trans-Australia Airlines provided us with free air travel to the Center and back.

To all of these people, and the many others who have helped us in a variety of ways, my wife and I extend our sincere thanks.

My own thanks are due to my wife who, as co-experimenter and tireless, enthusiastic worker, made the research itself and the writing of this report a special pleasure.

R.R.

Living Magic

CHAPTER 1

Living Magic

It was New Year's Day. Central Australia throbbed in the dull heat. The sun scorched the burnished countryside—the bare red hills of the MacDonnell Ranges fringing the township of Alice Springs, the brown sandy banks of the Todd River, the dusty streets. Groups of people, aborigines and whites, chatted listlessly in the meager shade.

Outside the hotel stood a three-ton truck. It was heavily laden with stores, and on top of the stores was a collection of about twenty aborigines—men, women, and children—laughing happily and enjoying the rare luxury of ice-cold soft drinks. As bottles were passed from one to the other and emptied, fresh bottles were produced. These all went to a big, bright-eyed native, incongruously named Cyril, who put the tops of the bottles to his mouth and lifted off the caps with his teeth.

At the wheel of the truck was Stanley, a slim, shy full blood. My wife, Lyn, and a young white woman going out to Hermannsburg as a nurse to the hundreds of natives centered about the mission there, sat beside Stanley in the cab. I scrambled onto the stores at the back and found a more or less comfortable place between Cyril and a lad of about fourteen who held a rifle across his bare knees.

Before us lay the barren but colorful plains to Hermanns-burg, and from there (our headquarters) the investigation of magic among tribal aborigines.

Lyn and I had been interested in magic for some time—not the medieval sort with witches, bubbling caldrons, and the like, but the magic being practiced by primitive peoples in the world today.

We wanted to find out if the accounts of aborigines dying as a result of being "pointed" with a bone had any foundation in fact; whether recovery after treatment by an aboriginal "clever-man" or doctor was relevant to modern ideas about psychosomatic medicine.

We were seeking the truth underlying accounts indicating that natives had some power white people would call tele-pathic, which enabled them to know what was happening to friends and relatives perhaps a hundred miles away. Ac-counts from a wide variety of sources, some of them appar-ently reliable, said that natives would travel great distances prompted by mysterious hunches.

And there were other problems, too: like that of sorting out these occurrences from mere superstitions and queer be-liefs. This problem had been dramatically illustrated by a knowledgeable prospector we had met in Alice Springs a few days before.

The prospector had just come into "the Alice" after months in the Haatz Range to the east, seeking opals.

"Yes, they're funny people," he said. "You've heard about the old fellow at Hermannsburg, I suppose. Worked in the tannery they have there. Well, one morning he came to work and went round to all his workmates, shaking hands with them. They couldn't make him out, as he hadn't done any-thing like this before.

"To each and every one of them the old fellow said he was glad to have worked with them and hoped that he wouldn't be forgotten by them. That evening they found him seated by the old church at the mission, dead. Looks like the old fellow knew his time was up, doesn't it?

"And they're a superstitious lot," the prospector went on, "even though they sometimes send a chill up m' spine with some of the things they seem to know, about what's going on.

"Take my boys, f'rinstance. One of 'em there, 'Ten-Bob Harry,' is what they call clever. Seems to go into trances and tells the other fellow, Undaria, that he's been travelin' round the countryside in spirit form seeing that his people are all right.

"I don't know. I leave it to the anthropologists. Thing that puzzles me is this, though—they can give you goose pimples with some of the things they seem to know, particularly these clever ones who almost make you think they're godlike in some ways; and mixed up with all this is the queerest lot of mumbo-jumbo, obvious superstitious nonsense, that you could imagine.

"Take the Gringai, f'rinstance. Suppose one of them is on 'walkabout' and he's making bad time. He's afraid he won't reach his destination by nightfall, doesn't want to camp, so what does he do? He looks about for a mighty big round stone, and when he finds one he puts it in the fork of a tree, an' goes on his way confident the sun won't set before he gets where he's going."

The symbolism of this action, holding the sun to prevent it setting, was obvious. But it was not magical since the essence of magic is its intended practicality. Apparently the symbolism so often found in magic had been carried over to this superstition.

"Right down south, too," the prospector continued, "the Wotjobaluk, extinct now as a tribe, I suppose, thought that if one of 'em pointed at a rainbow without going through some silly rigmarole, his fingers would become crooked and contracted and he wouldn't be able to use his hands to make secret *corroboree* markings. Ah, I remember now—they could point at a rainbow only if they turned their fingers over each other, the second over the first, the third over the second, and so on.

"And take this fellow of mine, 'Ten-Bob Harry' the clever one. He told me once that he was on some magical expedition when the enemy tribe surprised him. Seems he thought he was chockablock full of magic at the time, so to avoid capture, he says, he turned himself into a snake and wriggled away!"

The old man laughed and showed a full set of perfect but tobacco-stained teeth.

"Makes you think, doesn't it? They believe things like that, it seems. They tell you, all serious, that some of their doctors can get up into the clouds, take them wherever they need rain."

"'Rides in the whirlwind and directs the storm.'" Lyn quoted Addison.

"That's right. And, as I say, mixed up with all the queer beliefs like this you get instances where it looks like they know more about the mind than we do."

The prospector brought out a pipe and settled back in his chair.

"A few years back I had a boy out in the hills with me—a Pitta Pitta—more than a hundred miles from his tribal country. Well, one day he was restless, couldn't work, seemed listless, half-dazed; I remember wondering if he'd caught some disease—things like measles hit these poor blighters pretty hard, y'know—didn't answer me a couple of times when I spoke to him. That night he said, 'I'm going to my people, boss.' I know they do get pretty lonely away from their tribe, but I thought it was more than just that so I asked him. Well, y'know, he told me that that day his father had died.

"Don't mind telling you, I felt spooky. Here was this fellow, a hundred miles from his home, and apparently knowing what was going on there. And that's not all. A couple of weeks

later I found out that he'd been right. His father had died—
bitten by a snake that day. Work that one out!"

The prospecter seemed surprised to know that white people occasionally have such experiences, especially where the
death or serious illness of a relative is involved, and that some
well-authenticated cases had been recorded.

"Bet they don't have the same utter conviction as the aborigines," he commented with some finality.

"Yes, generally speaking, you're right," I replied. "But there
are some exceptions. These psychic hunches, if you like to
call them that, are often dismissed from white people's minds,
almost before they register, because they can't be explained
rationally, or else they're swamped by other experiences. Besides, we have a very materialistic culture, not given much to
introspection, on the whole, whereas the aborigines are an
extremely contemplative people. Sometimes I think they can
see within themselves with a far deeper understanding than
we can."

The prospector's experiences and attitude toward them
were, we found, fairly typical of white people who have been
closely associated with aborigines over a lengthy period.

Anthropologists, too, had recorded accounts that remained
a challenge. One such instance recorded by Professor A. P.
Elkin, for example, was this: "A Nyul-Nyul informant told me
how he doubted the claim of a medicine man . . . . so to
test him, asked him to ascertain when his [the questioner's]
white employer was returning. He said that neither he nor
the medicine man knew this. The latter went off a short distance and sat under a tree with the moonlight playing through
the leaves, and produced his 'spirit-dogs' which he, the questioner, actually saw. The medicine man sent these familiars
on their errand, and some time later told him that as dawn
came next morning he would hear the sound of his employer's horse approaching. Sure enough, this came to pass, confounding the unbelief of my informant."

This was but one of many accounts. They varied in nature and in impressiveness, but they came from the length and breadth of aboriginal Australia, and had been collected from full-blooded tribal natives who had had the barest contact with white culture as well as from sophisticated light-castes, some of whom had never known tribal life.

My wife and I had indeed collected numbers of such accounts among detribalized aborigines on the north coast of New South Wales. For example, Frank Mitchell, a full-blooded Minyung (Queensland) native living on the government station at Woodenbong, had had a number of unusual experiences. We were told of one that had occurred about three weeks before, by the then manager of the station, Mr. J. Foster.

"Frank's small son was in Kyogle Hospital," said Mr. Foster. "He had been there for some time, and as far as I knew was not in a dangerous condition. One morning a few weeks ago Frank came to my residence here before breakfast. 'What's the matter, Frank?' I asked, and he told me that Billie had died in the hospital during the night. There is no way he could have known this—Kyogle Hospital is over forty miles away and my residence is the only place with a phone. I didn't know what to make of Frank's statement; I told him I'd ring the hospital later to reassure him. But before I had done so, my phone rang. It was Kyogle Hospital; they told me that Frank's son had suddenly taken a turn for the worse and had died during the night."

Later Lyn and I discussed this experience with the native. He said that he and his wife had been lying in bed in their shack on the station when he heard faltering footsteps on the veranda. These he recognized as the spirit footsteps of his deceased mother, and he heard the familiar tapping of her walking stick. His wife, Eileen, also heard these noises, as well as tapping on the windowpane. They interpreted these as "death signs" and concluded that little Billie had died.

"Frank is an interesting fellow," went on the manager. "He

had another one of these strange experiences only a couple of days ago. He came down to my residence in the early evening and said he wanted permission to leave—all natives have to report on and off the settlement. He said he was going to catch the evening bus to Brisbane—a hundred miles north—as his brother there was dying. He said he felt his brother would not last the night out.

"Well, after the episode of little Billie, I took Frank more seriously, although I thought the first time might have been a mere coincidence. Frank caught the evening bus at about seven. Each time the phone rang I half expected confirmation of his story, but it didn't come till the next morning. Then there was a telegram from Brisbane announcing that Frank's brother had died during the night. Frank probably reached his brother's side just before he died. Strange, isn't it!"

It was more than strange, we thought. Some of the material that had been gathered was downright uncanny. But so are some of the experiences that white people occasionally have.

One of the noteworthy things to us was that despite the vast differences in the two cultures, a thread of similarity ran through accounts recorded in each. Frank Mitchell's experiences, for example, paralleled, in their essential form, scores of well-documented cases recorded in civilized societies.

This was to be expected, of course, since human beings are fundamentally alike. The recorded accounts suggested, however, that the aborigines' experiences were more common, more vivid, and more compelling.

The similarities in the pattern were there, but aboriginal magic had additional features demanding investigation that would more than establish the common features. Some aspects, it seemed, could only be explained by farfetched hypotheses: Telepathy of a form and quality far exceeding that known to occur among whites was an explanation advanced; for in the aborigines telepathy seemed to be under conscious control and it was claimed that clever-men could read minds at will. Mass hypnotism far superior to that produced by white practitioners was suggested as responsible for other phenomena. Some investigators had advanced no explanation, and sheer magic would be necessary to explain many of the accounts they had recorded.

The problem of investigating aboriginal magic was far more complicated than merely deciding on a few elucidating techniques, Lyn and I found. In Central Australia, as on the coast, we were to find magic to be living; it was an integral part of aboriginal culture and, moreover, the very core of their secret life.

Aborigines generally are most reluctant to discuss even mundane aspects of their existence until they know the investigator intimately; esoteric aspects of their culture they guard sedulously.

They are timid in the extreme. They would, some careless investigators have found, rather "go bush" than submit to peremptory examination—more than one anthropologist or psychologist has found a camp or settlement deserted at his approach. To gain an understanding of the aborigines, the field worker has first to solve the problem of gaining their confidence. Having won their co-operation, the way is easier, but always it has to be borne in mind that they have a vastly different viewpoint from ours.

Nowhere have magic and psychical experience developed to such an extent, especially in relation to materialistic culture, as with these people. They still bear the stigma placed on them by William Dampier, who called them, in 1699, "the most miserable people in the world." It is true that this might well be the impression of the uninformed observer; yet even others have passed similar judgment on them. But people who have lived in close association with the aborigines, who have seen something of the richness and intensity of their contemplative existence, have found that their culture has qualities that in many ways make it admirable, and in some ways not greatly inferior, by comparison, to our own.

The aborigines have developed the art of contemplation to a degree that we cannot appreciate or even understand. Their whole way of life is patterned on concepts of rigid mental discipline. Their outlook is continuously and consistently toward the enhancement of the personality. Tribal natives go through life with the minimum of material possessions—no clothes, no wealth, no permanent dwellings—with a racial serenity that, to those who have attempted sympathetically to understand them, is mystifying and impressive.

Our problem was largely to bring reality and matter-of-factness to the mysteries of this culture. We decided to approach the problem in a number of different ways.

We first had to get the natives to talk about their magic, to describe their experiences, advance their own explanations of them, and gradually, we hoped, admit us to a considerable amount of their esoteric lore. We would thus continue a more or less traditional approach—that is, the recording of anecdotal accounts. However, this approach would be different in these respects: always we would be seeking the reality underlying the situation and looking for features common with the pattern of white people's similar experiences.

The recording of such accounts was soon systematized in a questionnaire that fairly exhaustively inquired into the major aspects of magic and psychical experience. The questionnaire itself produced a great deal of anecdotal material, for it served to remind native subjects of incidents they might easily have overlooked in an ordinary conversational inquiry. The main value of the questionnaire was that it gave us statistical information. We could say, within certain limits of accuracy, what proportion of a group of natives had had certain experiences, actually seen a magic cord, for example.

The most fruitful approach we expected to be in our experimental techniques. Some of these—certain psychological tests—could only be applied to the detribalized groups; others were taken from the laboratories of the parapsychologist, and with our adaptations of them could be applied to tribal people as well.

These tests were of two types. One was a card-guessing technique used to test extrasensory perception. With it we hoped to establish whether or not telepathy or anything akin to telepathy had any part in aboriginal magic. The other test involved the throwing of colored cubes or dice and was designed to test the effect, if any, of "willing" in certain aspects of magic.

We had already carried out thousands of card-guessing and dice-throwing tests and achieved results in some cases that were clear-cut and unequivocal. The tests were the first of this type to have been carried out with native peoples anywhere. In addition, we included in our program some tests of suggestibility and planned the hypnotizing of aboriginal subjects.

The techniques had been tried out so far only with the coastal people; their real trial was to be with the tribal natives of the desert. Some of the mystery had already been dispelled. We had found a core of reality and a hint that the explanation of aboriginal magic was understandable and fundamentally simple. But what fresh problems lay ahead of us?

We had little time for contemplation as we drove across the bare plains. Stanley was a good, fast driver. The miles slipped by and we passed through scorched, red country, beautiful in its austere and lonely grandeur. Here and there bright patches of green relieved the crimsons and siennas, for the Center had just had heavy rains, the first for three years. The ragged mountain ranges cut into the deep blue, clear sky.

Forty miles out we approached a patch of brighter and denser greenness.

"Strehlow's camp," said Cyril. Strehlow, an early Lutheran

missionary and anthropologist, had made his camp here at Jay's Creek.

Today, being New Year's Day, was a gala occasion for the small group of natives living at the creek, we found. Twenty or thirty of them were gathered about a group of galvanized-iron buildings. It was their annual race day. The field: two horses!

We waited for a few minutes and watched the race of the day; then, since the shadows were already beginning to lengthen, we pushed on.

As the sun sank lower, we began to see groups of kangaroos in the distance and dozens of rabbits appeared by the side of the road. We took pot shots at them with the fourteen-year-old's rifle, but the speed of the truck and the roughness of the road gave them immunity. Stanley was, however, after bigger game.

Suddenly he cut the motor and the truck glided to a standstill.

"'Roo," whispered Cyril, and pointed out a magnificent kangaroo, fully six feet tall, standing immobile a couple of hundred yards away. Quietly Stanley took a .303 rifle from the cab of the truck and, walking a few yards toward the animal, dropped to one knee, took careful aim, and fired.

The crack shattered the still air. The kangaroo made a few, frantic leaps and then dropped.

With wild whoops the children swarmed off the truck and raced across to the dead animal. In a few minutes it had been hauled back to the truck and trussed onto the front bumper.

Half a mile farther on Stanley offered me a shot at another 'roo. I missed, but, taking the rifle from me, Stanley sighted after the fleeing animal and dropped it. It was a splendid shot in the failing light.

Several times we crossed swollen creeks. Often Stanley got out and, pulling up his trousers, tested the ford before we crossed. Night had fallen when we came to the last crossing. The water swept over Stanley's knees before he was halfway across, and he would not risk the crossing.

Slowly, cautiously, he drove along the bank for about half a mile and explored another crossing. I got down from the truck and, with the aboriginal youngsters, started to wade to the other side. But the pebbles bruised my tender feet and I slipped, plunging into the stream. There were shrieks of merriment from the children.

Cyril splashed over to me and helped me to my feet. "Catch any fish?" he asked with a grin.

On the far side of the creek the children began to make tiny fires—just a few leaves and twigs—and marked a track for the truck to return to the road farther upstream. Stanley drove across and we piled on board again.

Near the bank was a camp fire. Beside it, completely naked, stood an aboriginal stockman, his skin gleaming black with kangaroo fat. He waved a cheery greeting.

We approached Hermannsburg in the dead of the night. The natives on the back of the truck became restless as a few lights came into view on the horizon; they were lanterns of the missionaries and a few scattered native fires. Stanley began to toot the horn.

Suddenly we were in the mission compound, the truck spurting up vast clouds of powdery dust. As we came to a standstill, the truck was surrounded by dozens of excited natives. The kangaroos were unroped and carried off to be quickly cooked and eaten. There were one or two white children from the mission there, too, talking fluently in the native tongue.

Soon Lyn and I had our gear unpacked and beds roughly arranged on an open veranda. As we prepared to settle down for the night, we could hear in the distance animated talking around the camp fires. From the far distance came the dull "boom boom" of a ceremonial bull-roarer, and we thought we heard the plaintive notes of a *didjeridoo,* a very primitive native wind instrument.

This was Australia's "dead heart."

Cyril passed by and we called him over. "What's going on, Cyril?" we asked.

"It's them Pitjendadjara," he replied. "Fellow name of Tjal-kalieri making *corroboree.*"

CHAPTER 2

Sorcery

Tjalkalieri squatted among the red sand hills near the Hermannsburg Mission in Central Australia, talking about the magic of his tribe.

He was a Pitjendadjara of full blood, in his early forties I thought, intelligent, co-operative, steeped in aboriginal lore: he was, indeed, a tribal elder. Dressed in ill-fitting western clothes, loose, laceless boots with no socks, and an old hat, he looked a little like Charlie Chaplin. But stripped, wearing his initiate's headband, a thin white bone through the pierced septum of his nose, he was a magnificent, almost terrifying, specimen of vigorous manhood.

He had two wives. The second, younger wife had been forced on him (he said) by pressure from his tribe, and despite opposition from the mission. His home was now at the Lutheran mission here at Hermannsburg; he, his two wives, three children, and a number of scrawny dogs lived in a tiny bark shelter near the banks of the Finke River. One of the children was not his (his first wife had had a temporary association with a white man) but he loved the "half-caste kid," as he called Nugget, as tenderly as those he had fathered himself.

The mission would have preferred him to be back in his rugged tribal country in the Petermann Ranges to the west, this man and his two wives. But if he went, if he were compelled to go, the rest of the Pitjendadjara people there would go, too. So he stayed.

We had been talking about bone pointing, a ritualistic form of sorcery.

Taking a handful of red sand, Tjalkalieri let it trickle out through his fingers. Partly in broken English, partly in his native tongue, he said: "A man's life goes away like the sand, sometimes fast, sometimes slow. But when a man is pointed his life is finished." He opened his hand wide and the sand emptied from it.

A faint breeze stirred the burning sand dunes and the spinifex rustled stiffly. Beads of perspiration stood out on the native's forehead.

"Finished," he repeated, and smoothed the sand in front of him as if to make his meaning clearer, more emphatic.

This is what the accounts had said—the stories told by cattlemen and travelers who had encountered tribal or nearly tribal aborigines, and the carefully recorded statements of anthropologists—when a man is pointed he dies.

To Tjalkalieri it was as simple as that; to my wife and me who had come to the Red Center to investigate aboriginal magic, it was one of the most extraordinary human problems in the world today.

It had not been easy to induce Tjalkalieri to talk about magic, particularly of such deadly forms as bone pointing. He did not talk freely to my wife about magic though he went farther with her than he would have dared to do with a native woman. A female white investigator among the aborigines is a sort of neuter gender.

Daily we two men had left her and wandered off by ourselves to the sand dunes near the mission. There the story began to unfold. Tjalkalieri talked about love magic, with a merry twinkle in his eyes; about the strange ways in which the clever-men of his tribe, the doctors, could cure illnesses by sucking their patients' bodies; he told how rain is made in this parched homeland of his; and then he talked about black magic—bone pointing, the *kurdaitcha* shoes, the magic cord that could issue forth from a magician and strike a man down with its invisible power.

"What does a bone look like?"

"I knew you would want to know." He fished awkwardly in the pocket of his loose coat, through a hole in the pocket and into the lining, and brought forth this most deadly of aboriginal magic weapons.

It was slender and white, made from a forearm bone of a dead woman, he said, about nine inches long and ground to a fine point at one end. At the other end was a blob of black, resinous substance resembling pitch. This, he told me, came from spinifex bushes.

How was it made?

Quickly he gathered an armful of drying spinifex, put it in a heap, and beat it with a stick. Then, with borrowed matches, he set fire to it. As it burned he gathered the ashes into a tiny heap. When the fire had died down, he puffed away the ashes and gathered up the residue—a tiny ball of pliable black substance that he kneaded between his fingers. He was making the desert natives' cement.

"When it is cold it is very hard," he said.

Stuck to the bone with this spinifex gum was a cord of finely plaited human hair—a woman's hair, Tjalkalieri explained, for each man is entitled to his wife's mother's hair to make the cord. This cord was about three feet long and rather lightish brown in color, for aborigines' hair is not black. Young children in the Center usually have tawny hair that darkens as they grow older.

There it lay in his hand—a small human bone, a cord of human hair, a weapon.

"Show me how it is pointed."

A strange expression lit the native's face. He gripped the

bone in his left hand and took the cord in his right. He struck a pose and became immobile.

Reaching for my camera, I said, "Point it at me."

"No."

"No?"

"Not at you."

"Why not?"

Flatteringly he explained that he did not wish to kill me.

I had not expected this explanation, for I knew that although the pointing bone was a potent weapon, it usually had to be "loaded" in a special ceremony during which sacred and secret songs were sung and rituals performed.

"Tjalkalieri," I said, "surely it is not loaded. Surely it is not ready for a killing."

"It is loaded," he replied, with a grim smile, and I thought his features relaxed a little. "It is always loaded, this one."

Then he explained. "The doctor who made this bone was very strong. As he made it he sang his song—his own song of power. The strength in him passed along his fingers, into the bone, into the cord. It is part of him, and it is as strong as he was. This is a killer, this one."

There was no doubt he believed the bone could kill. The sand dunes seemed to echo the sincerity of his words: "This is a killer, this one." Suddenly the desert felt chill.

The explanation that a bone absorbed its maker's power was then a new one to me; the utter, simple belief in the power of these psychic weapons to kill was not. All tribal aborigines, and even light-caste, detribalized natives, believe in the power of a pointed bone to kill—in the hands of a skilled practitioner of magic.

I felt tempted to challenge this solemn brown man squatting in the sand before me, to tell him I did not believe that the bone could harm me, but I did not do so, for two reasons.

First, it would have strained the bond of sympathy between us, the bond my wife and I had so carefully built up over the preceding weeks in the desert. We had tried to get these people to open their hearts, talk frankly and freely about their magic, to clear the way for the tests we were later to apply. We had not laughed at the aborigines' beliefs. We had solemnly discussed, as though they had been matters of sober fact, natives' descriptions of their clever-men, how they could ride through the heavens in storms, travel vast distances in no time, foretell the future, commune with the spirits of the dead. I did not challenge Tjalkalieri because the bond was vital to our investigation. Secondly, I did not challenge him because I respected him as a man.

"You are right, Tjalkalieri. I would not point a loaded rifle at you," I said.

He leaned forward and clasped my hand. It was one of those simple gestures for which neither his tongue nor mine had words. We lapsed into reverie.

Less than a mile to the west of us lay the sprawling white buildings of the Lutheran mission, beyond them the salty trickle that was the Finke, and then, pinked by the setting sun, the magnificent, spinifex-studded walls of the Finke Gorge. Idly our eyes wandered over the scene—the bare, dusty cattle yards, empty now because the three thousand head of stock supervised by half a dozen dusky Aranda stock-men and a white overseer were scattered over the camp of the Pitjendadjara, Tjalkalieri's people; a dozen or more scattered bark, grass, and canvas shelters, with an occasional camp fire throwing a thin silver stream into the clear sky; a few naked children laughing happily, some playing their traditional games; native women tardily preparing the evening meal of damper; and, coming over the skyline, a lone hunter. Tjalkalieri shaded his eyes and then answered my unasked question. "Yes, it is Maleiaba—with a fine euro."

(Euros, marsupials resembling kangaroos, but smaller, originally abounded in this area, but are now rare close to the mission.)

There was a hum of activity around the mission buildings, too. The bell of the church which stood in the center of the buildings, in a square where the sand had been turned to dust, had sounded. The old men, men of the Aranda tribe, had ceased their games of marbles and trooped bareheaded into the simple church. The pastor walked slowly across the yard.

To the right of the missioners' homes was the Aranda camp—disorderly rows of small, galvanized-iron buildings— the present home of the Aranda, once the greatest and noblest tribe to hunt the Center.

Tjalkalieri was perhaps thinking of his own tribal country to the west, a huge area bounded roughly by the Ayers Rock, the largest rock in the world, on its eastern side and extending westward into the Petermann Ranges. His people still lived there in much the same way as they had before the white man had come. Perhaps he was thinking of the great mythological heroes who sanctified the tribal magic, and of the Dream Time whence most of his tribe's traditions came.

I was still thinking of the pointing bone that lay in the sand beside him, and of its mysterious powers. The power did not lie in the bone itself, that was certain. Did it lie in the operator? Or in the victim? The essential facts were simple enough, for a few cases of bone pointing had been investigated by white doctors. The victims had been found to be organically sound, yet they had died. Suggestion? The aborigines are a suggestible, superstitious people—at least they seem to be on the surface. But what sort of suggestion is it that can kill a man?

Perhaps I had thought aloud, uttered a quiet, incredulous, "How?"

"It is like a spear of thought," said my companion. I had not expected such a penetrating observation. Usually only the ritual was described. This man with me was an unusually keen psychologist.

If a native knows he has been pointed, does he will himself to death—in a few hours, at most a few days? If we civilized people want to kill ourselves, we must take physical action against ourselves with firearms or poisons. Could a native take psychical action against himself, kill himself with his own thoughts? Or could curses kill? How little we know about the human mind, after all. Dare we scoff at the Australian aborigines' belief in a "spear of thought"?

So many questions.

"This spear of thought, how does it work? What does the clever-man do?" I asked.

Tjalkalieri described something of the ritual, something of the belief underlying it. Ordinarily, he said, a bone has to be "loaded" before it has the power to kill; often a bone is made especially for a particular killing. Sometimes the sorcerer acts for himself alone, sometimes for the tribe or section of the tribe. In the loading ceremony ancient tribal songs are sung and the clever-men infuse some of their power into the bone. Sometimes in these ceremonies the clever-men give psychical displays, climbing to the tops of trees with the help of magic cords that they can make exude from the navel or mouth. He had seen this.

When the bone is ready the man selected as the killer goes off, perhaps with one or two companions, into the bush. He takes up a ritually sanctioned pose and points and jerks the bone in the direction of his intended victim. Usually he mutters a chant over it.

I had read of such songs. Some were recorded by Spencer and Gillen, early workers in this very area. One chant of the Aranda people was simply a series of curses. Translated, it went:

> "May your heart be rent asunder.
> May your backbone be split open
> and your ribs torn asunder.
> May your head and throat be split open."

The pointing, Tjalkalieri continued, was but the first part of the killing. The shadow, or psychical counterpart, had, if the magic had been well and truly done, entered the victim's body. Thus, according to the theory of the natives, there were two bones now—one held by the killer, the other in the victim's body. Whatever happened to the first bone would happen to the other.

Now we were on more familiar ground. This was imitative magic, found in a variety of guises from ancient times to the present, and in the present among primitive people the world over. This is the sort of magic involved when a wax or clay image is pierced and the person of whom it is the likeness is believed to suffer pain or die.

The aboriginal sorcerer, Tjalkalieri continued, is now ready to complete his task. Usually he delays this till the following day when he has returned to camp and the word is whispered around that the particular person has been pointed.

"Then the person who has been pointed always knows it?" I asked. This was a vital question. However little we may know about suggestion, it made this the more likely explanation if the intended victim knew of the fate planned for him.

"Yes."

"What happens then?"

"The bone is burned. The other bone in the man sears his heart. He is ready to die. The songs of power are sung again. Already he is sick. There is death in the man and he knows it. Soon he will die. His relatives mourn him. All the people mourn him."

"Before he is dead?"

"There is death in the man."

If this were suggestion, what power it has among these simple people! The accounts said that after a pointing a man might live only a day, perhaps only hours. With his people already mourning him as dead, the psychological pressure on the victim is tremendous. Was there no escape, no remedy?

Yes, conceded Tjalkalieri, if a doctor, a very great and powerful doctor, stronger than the sorcerer and willing to pit himself against him, could be induced to attempt the cure. About this he would tell me tomorrow.

This was the signal to return to camp, he to his two wives in his bark shelter, I to the quarters provided by the mission for our stay in the area. As we walked slowly back to the area, this native whom the missionaries called "Tiger," for his name means tiger cat, talked about some of the less grave aspects of pointing the bone.

There were many sorts of bones. Some he would show me tomorrow. His neighbors, the Loritja, used a strange type. Loritja was not the name of a tribe, he told me, but meant "westerners" or "foreigners." The people of whom he spoke used a pointing bone similar to the one he had shown me, but which had a set of eagle's claws attached by means of spinifex gum to the pointing end. Thus, when the bone—that is, the spirit form of the bone—entered the victim's body, the claws would crush and tear out his heart. Another, similar bone required two men to point it. It was actually made up of five bones. These were held by one man. They converged to a point and joined to a human hair cord. On the other end of the cord, held by the second native, were the eagle talons.

"Must you always use a bone for your pointing?" I asked. I had heard that among tribes in fairly close contact with white culture some strange variants had been discovered. Investigators had found discarded rifle barrels or sheets of tin used in one area, an indication that the bone or its equivalent was not thought by the natives to be vital to the killing process but was only a symbol. The power was with the operator—or with the victim—to make the killing process effective.

As I asked the question my mind went back to a similar conversation I had had some months before. On this occasion my informant had not been an unsophisticated tribal native, who still participated in age-old rituals, who hunted with spear and boomerang, who wore clothes only when he visited a mission settlement or an outback station. My informant then was an old man who had lived for forty or more years in or near towns and cities. His tribe, the Birri, had had their tribal area near Bowen, in Queensland, and had long since broken up. He was a native who had lived in the white man's ways for many years, but whose belief in magic was as profound as Tjalkalieri's. He had told me a story of how a man had been pointed and how he had died. His story was unusual in two respects: the man in this case probably did not know that he had been pointed, though he might have guessed it; and the sorcerer who had performed the killing showed, apparently, an extraordinary, inexplicable, knowledge of the efficacy of his magic.

This was the story as told me by Harry Monsell: "Many years ago, when I was a young man, the law was broken in my tribe. A man who should not have done so—for he had gone through the 'rule' [been initiated] and knew it was wrong and against the will of the people—took two girls off into the bush. The girls did not go willingly, but he had threatened them, and as it was said that he was clever, the girls went with him. They were afraid of his magic.

"He should not have used his cleverness for a thing like this. The people were angry and the elders spoke of what should be done. Some said that they should track him, catch him, and spear him. Others thought all three should be punished. One old fellow, the cleverest of the doctors, had his way. He said that he would point the man and kill him.

"The old fellow—he had white hair and a white beard and could hardly walk—took a piece of fencing wire. It was about a foot long. He took one of his clever stones and with it he beat one end of the wire into a point. On the other end of the wire he attached a piece of wax from a nest of wild bees.

"He went a little way away from the main camp. Then he sat down and sang the curses of the man who broke the law, pointing and jerking the 'bone' first one way then another.

"Every night he did this at his camp fire, a short distance from the main camp of the tribe. He held the 'bone' over the fire and it became very hot; and every night he sang the 'bone' away into the bush seeking out the man who had taken the two girls.

"For more than a week he did this, while the old men looked and the women hid their heads.

"Then one night he put the 'bone' down and said: 'I got that fellow.'

"Two days later the girls came back to the tribe. They told us that the man had said he felt sick. After a few days he had had to lie down most of the day and then, at about the time the old clever-man had said he got him, he had died.

"The doctors of my tribe were pretty strong in the old days."

While I was thinking over old Harry Monsell's story and the use of a piece of fencing wire for pointing, Tjalkalieri spoke.

"You asked a question—is there anything but a bone can be used for pointing? Often an old clever-man uses a stone, one of his clever stones. He puts a cord on it and uses it in the same way as an ordinary bone."

Tjalkalieri then described a curious form of pointing that he had heard about, but not seen. It could only be performed by very powerful doctors, and if a doctor were powerful enough to use it, it was very effective. The doctor merely moistened the tip of his index finger at his lips, thereby presumably taking some of the power that doctors are supposed to have, and walking straight to his intended victim, he pointed his finger at him and uttered his name. The natives called this "spittle-throwing." This indeed must be a terrifying experience for the intended victim, and it is not surprising that, if suggestion be responsible for pointing-bone deaths, it is so effective in these circumstances.

This is probably the simplest method of pointing that there is. Often, in the ordinary pointing ceremonies, such things as the nature of the terrain must be taken into account. If there is a water hole between the pointer and the pointed, for example, the sorcery may be rendered ineffective. Usually, too, the pointer must ensure that the sun or the moon is directly behind him and projecting his shadow in the direction of the intended victim. This is supposed to aid the shadow of the pointing bone as it flies to its mark.

Pointing apparatus is used ritually to "kill" novices in initiation ceremonies or aspiring doctors in the doctor-making rituals. As an instrument it may be used against simple enemies to avenge a real or supposed wrong or insult, against those who have violated tribal law, adulterers, or as a demonstration and a threat to a group or more usually to an individual. It is used by individuals against individuals, and by groups against groups. Sometimes a pointing is sanctioned or carried out by tribal elders; at other times it may be a secretive (and rather dangerous) affair.

"I have heard, too," said Tjalkalieri, "of a doctor who could throw one of his clever stones so that it went into a man without leaving a mark. The stone would make the man very sick. If the doctor sang a song, he made the stone hot so that it hurt or killed the man. Some time later the stone comes back to the doctor. Then he looks at it, and if it has got blood on it, he knows the man is dead."

On the following day Tjalkalieri brought with him Maleiaba, his kinsman from the Ayers Rock area. For an aboriginal, Maleiaba was unusually short—about five feet. But, although well over sixty, he was solidly built and powerful. It was customary for him to walk twenty miles in one day over the rough country around the Finke, out toward Palm Valley, spend perhaps an hour in the careful stalking of a euro or kangaroo, as he had done the day before, and return the miles to camp with it slung over his shoulder. But he was bald, and his baldness was a constant source of embarrassment to him, so he almost always wore a battered hat to hide his shame. He wore his hat even when he stripped off his western clothes to "go walkabout" or to hunt. (Going walkabout is concerned partly with ritual travel over the tribal area, and is partly an urge to be constantly on the move. Even natives living near the cities often go walkabout.)

I had seen him use his spear and *woomera* (spear thrower). With them he could put a spear right through the body of a kangaroo at fifty yards. He had his spear and *woomera* with him now, and in the hollow of the *woomera* he carried some objects I could not see.

Silently we three walked through the spinifex toward the sand hills. Ceaselessly the natives' eyes wandered over the sands before us, reading their silent message. Occasionally there was a brief explanation, interpreting for me the marks they saw. "Snake, big fellow, poison." "Perentie." "Anana [a tribesman] go along here."

We chose a spot to rest. There was no shade, but the natives were used to the merciless sun. Tjalkalieri and I sat down. Swiftly Maleiaba walked on fifty yards or so and circled us. It was a precaution, I learned, against women overhearing what we were to talk about and seeing what they had brought to show me.

First Tjalkalieri produced from his coat a pointing bone similar to the one I had seen the previous day.

"This is a pointer of the Pitta Pitta people." This was a neighboring tribe. The bone, a kangaroo bone in this case, was roughly carved. Lines of varying width cut into its surface, encircling it, and there were whorls spiraling down to the point. It was not an intricate piece of carving but, considering that the craftsman's tool had been nothing more than a flaked and chipped stone, a primitive chisel, it was a remarkable piece of work.

Beside it Tjalkalieri placed another bone. This was most ornately decorated with white down from a cockatoo. Some of the down was stained red, and I noticed that all of it was attached to the bone with a red substance.

"Blood," said Tjalkalieri. And, touching his arm, added, "My blood." He went on to say that he and Maleiaba had made the bone the previous night, to show me. They had drawn the blood from his arm as they would have done if the bone had been intended for real use. This co-operation was typical of the aborigines if their friendship had been won. Once I had asked a native if there were any rock paintings in the area. There were none, he said. But on the following day I was surprised to see a black-and-white sacred snake painted onto the red-rock wall of a cave where we used to meet. It had been painted for my benefit. This occasional anxiousness of aborigines to so indulge the white man who gains their confidence is, however, a source of danger to the unwary investigator. In their desire to please, natives may pervert the truth and give the investigator the answer to his questions that they expect will please him. Thus it is necessary to check and cross-check statements against each other and from informant to informant.

The highly decorated bone, the Pitjendadjara men told me, was used in initiation ceremonies. The novice is "killed" by the bone and is then reborn into his life as an initiate of the tribe.

Yet another bone was produced by Tjalkalieri. This was a thin, bare, undecorated bone about six inches long. Carefully the native pushed it through the hole in the septum of his nose. This bone could be used for killing, too.

Just as a collector, proudly exhibiting his items, saves his most prized specimen for the last, so apparently had Tjalkalieri and Maleiaba. With a grunt Maleiaba turned to the *woomera* beside him and took from it two objects that looked rather like large bird nests. They were made of downy emu and cockatoo feathers held in shape by human blood and hair cord fashioned from the fur of kangaroos or euros. They were like big slippers, shoes.

I looked at my companions. Together they said, *"Kurdaitcha."*

Kurdaitcha, the most terrifying form of aboriginal sorcery, found in but a few areas, flourishes in the Center. I questioned the natives on the *kurdaitcha* ritual, its meaning and its explanation.

Kurdaitcha is a special form of magic, they told me, usually practiced at the behest of tribal headmen. The name refers both to the shoes and the ritual. The wearer of the shoes, that is, the native selected for the task of killing—and none must refuse on pain of death—has first to have his little toes dislocated in a special ceremony. This, according to the native's belief, makes his toes as eyes so that he does not stumble in the dark. The soft pad of the shoes effectively disguises a native's footprints (all tribal members are readily identifiable to others by their prints) and the dislocation of the toes distorts the wearer's gait, a trait that might easily give him away.

Sometimes *kurdaitcha* killers have as their object the stealing of a man's kidney fat. This is the ritualistic interpretation. It does not in fact occur. In most *kurdaitcha* killings, the natives said, the victim is killed, usually by spearing; then a clever-man who has accompanied the killing expedition performs a magical operation, sealing over the spear wound so that no mark shows on the native's skin, and temporarily restores him to life. After a day or two the native dies.

This is the aboriginal statement of what occurs. Probably what actually happens is that the victim is speared and dies. The doctor then goes through a ceremony (which is wholly symbolic in character or else he hypnotizes the members of the

42

party) in which he restores life and kills again, this time by magic. Thus he infuses mystery into what is probably a very ordinary killing, and makes it a thoroughly magical one.

A native of Tjalkalieri's tribe, Selly, was killed by *kurdaitcha* a short time ago for revealing tribal secrets to women. He was found with his neck broken.

"Your people are afraid of *kurdaitcha?*"

"They are afraid of all [black] magic. Besides these things a man must be careful that hairs that fall from his head, his fingernails and toenails are not found by another man who wants to harm him. This man can burn or sing the things that he finds and make their owner very sick."

This type of sorcery is world-wide. A new South Wales native, Tom Kenny, had not long before told me of an incident he had seen in his youth. A girl in his tribe had been wronged by a man, and she practiced magic against him. The girl obtained a small portion of the man's hair and nail parings and buried them in a spot a short distance from the camp. This spot she kept secret, but she told other members of the tribe what she had done and declared that as the hair and nail parings deteriorated, so the man would sicken and die. The native did in fact get sick and he sought the services of a tribal doctor. The doctor was able, Kenny said, with his clever eye to find the objects used by the girl in her magic. He obtained these, returned them to the man, cautioned him to be more careful in the future, rubbed his body, blew into his mouth, and the native recovered.

"You were going to tell me," I said to Tjalkalieri, "how a doctor can cure someone who has had a bone pointed at him."

"For *kurdaitcha* there is no cure. There is nothing for a doctor to take out. If a doctor points his finger at a man, there is nothing for another doctor to take out. For a man who has a bone in him there is hope—if the doctor is strong. Maleiaba came today and we will show you."

I then witnessed an extraordinary pantomime with these two natives playing the parts of pointing victim and doctor. The two Pitjendadjara men enjoyed their play immensely, roaring with laughter as they acted out, and at the same time explained, a native magical cure. There was no atmosphere of gloom as there probably would be in real life.

Tjalkalieri lay in the sand and clasped his hands over his abdomen. "There is a bone in me!" He moaned and groaned (and laughed); and his contortions whipped up the sand. "I am dying. The bone is tearing the insides of me." Then he said, "The great and clever doctor, Maleiaba—he, he, ho—will cure me! Oh, the pain, oh, ah!"

With serious face the little Ayers Rock man examined the writhing Tjalkalieri. He rubbed his abdomen, feeling carefully with the tips of his fingers. He applied his lips to the bare skin and pretended to suck. Tjalkalieri's contortions became less violent. Then Maleiaba felt again with his fingers and, with skillful sleight of hand, produced a short pointing bone (without wax and cord) apparently from the patient's abdomen. He held aloft with a grin of triumph.

"*Yokai!*" he cried.

"*Yokai!*" I echoed the Pitjendadjara equivalent of "Hooray!" and applauded his performance.

His patient was sitting up now with a broad smile lighting his features.

"Pretty good, eh? Now we do it again."

He lay down and the pantomime, act two, was resumed. "I am sick. I have been pointed. Inside me there is great troubles. It is a bone. The great—he, he—the great doctor—ho, ha—Maleiaba will take the bone from me and make me well."

The little ceremony of examining the patient, feeling, sucking, feeling again, was repeated. This time, however, with a solemn look darkening his face, Maleiaba produced

44

but half a bone, a fragment. Sadly he looked at the "dying" man.

"You will die. I am clever for I have taken half the bone. But your kinsmen in the Dream Time, the relatives who have gone before you, will let me take only part of the bone. They want you to come to them. You will die. Good-by, my friend, good-by. Say your farewells to your relatives and those you love, for you are to die."

Surprise, disappointment, resignation were pictured in Tjalkalieri's face. With a sly grin at me he said, "I am dying, farewell." His body stiffened. He opened one eye a little and whispered, "I am dead!"

The game was over; I congratulated them on their performance. Their little drama had told me a great deal: they had given me something of the atmosphere of such a curing procedure, a sight never witnessed by a white man. They had completed for me a picture, still inadequate for the central, basic facts were still unexplained, of the structure of sorcery among their people.

I pondered briefly on the social significance of sorcery. It is part of their law, for through it the tribal headmen mete out their justice. It is, too, a ready means of explaining the origin of illnesses (a native who falls ill from natural causes often blames magic); and it points the way to their cure through the healing powers of the native doctor. But what prestige the doctors must have to effect their cures, to change, often so dramatically, the nature of their patient's well-being!

As we walked slowly back to camp, my two dark companions' irrepressible sense of humor became evident again; they resumed the little play they had acted so brilliantly in the sand hills. Maleiaba pretended to extract bone after bone from Tjalkalieri's body—from his chest, his neck, his head, his abdomen. Each time they looked with apparent incredulity at the bone, examined it carefully to see that it was whole, and then together roared, "*Yokai!*"

I let their buffoonery go on for some time, and then I said, "Tjalkalieri, these doctors must be great and powerful men, who understand a man's mind."

He sobered instantly. "They see inside it just as they can see inside his body to find the bones."

"I wish," I said, "that I could meet some of these fellows."

"Then," replied Tjalkalieri, "you must come with me to my people in the valley at Areyonga."

Before we could discuss plans Maleiaba had produced yet another bone—this time from himself!

In unison all three of us yelled, "*Yokai!*"

CHAPTER 3

To Areyonga

"Woosh," said Kinchika. "Wooshta, woosh!" The camel snapped viciously at the boy's slender brown fingers, reared, and then plunged forward onto its front knees. "Woosh," he cried again, tugging at the rope, and one or two bloody spots glistened at the peg through the animal's nose. "Woosh." And the angry beast shuddered down to rest and became calm.

There were two camels in our team. The first was the riding camel, a cantankerous bull which, during the journey, turned its ugly head and snapped at my legs as I perched precariously in the front saddle. Lyn rode aft on the ship of the desert, behind the hump. The second camel, carrying the awkward camel boxes with our supplies, was a cow in an advanced stage of pregnancy. At Tjalkalieri's suggestion, for he had guided another white man before with a camel in similar condition, we called her "Lady-in-Waiting"—and hoped that she would wait till we had completed our journey to Areyonga.

Tjalkalieri came along as our camel man. He was glad to get away from the mission for a short time and visit his kinsmen in the valley. He had arranged the hire of the camels from a fellow tribesman visiting on walkabout from a nearby cattle station, and was bringing along Kinchika, a lad who he assured us was a "good boy." Tjalkalieri had traveled the aboriginal foot tracks to the deep valley in the Krichauff Ranges many times, but the camel path was new and unfamiliar to him. Kinchika, however, whose home was in the valley, had once traveled the path and he was to be our guide. No white man had been over this country before. There were Air Force maps of the area, but we found them so inaccurate they were soon discarded.

Tjalkalieri brought his little black mare which he and the boy rode alternately. The beast had wonderful stamina, despite its shaggy appearance, and stood up well to the desert crossing, the heat and lack of water.

When we first saw Kinchika we were surprised. He was no more than eleven years of age, and he stared at us solemnly through a thatch of wild brown hair that fell over his brow and hid most of his face. I suppose it acted as a sort of fly veil. During the couple of months he was with us he did not attempt to push the hair aside.

Already the boy's body was scarred with cicatrices, for his initiation had begun; his slim arms were disfigured with circular weals—burn marks. He had had to submit to glowing red wood coals being pushed into his flesh, and show no sign of pain. The major operation of his initiation, circumcision, had yet to be performed. Tjalkalieri told me that, a few years before, a sharp stone was the only instrument used for this, but contact with white people had had its effect and now "blazor rades" were used when they could be obtained.

The boy could handle camels almost as well as Tjalkalieri. The first hazard of the journey was to get the camels across the Finke. The river had been in flood following the greatest rains the Center had had for half a century. Coming from Adelaide by plane we had seen Lake Eyre and Lake Torrens, normally flat salt pans, filled and overflowing. The Finke still had water in it and, although this was but a foot deep, to get the camels across it was a major operation. Lyn and I had dismounted and crossed the stream on the little black mare. As we watched the camels, plunging and rearing while the two natives coaxed, cajoled, and threatened them, we could see that the journey would probably not be without incident.

Little groups of natives had gathered on the banks to watch our progress. The pastor came down and held an animated conversation with Tjalkalieri. Then he joined us.

"I've checked with Tiger on the route he proposes to take you," said the pastor, "and after evening service I'll radio Koschade in the valley to let him know you're on your way. Radio's more reliable than this aboriginal telegraphy or telepathy, or whatever it is you're playing around with, I say. Though I wouldn't be surprised if Tiger's people know he's on the way already.

"Water O.K.? Anyhow, after these rains you'll never be far from a water hole. After all, if holes are forty miles apart it means you're not more than twenty miles from water any time.

"Your camels look pretty rough, but the boys should be able to handle them for you. Tell them to watch that they don't eat the poison weed near Gilbert Springs. I've told Tiger, but in my forty years with these people I've yet to meet one who's thoroughly reliable. That fellow's got two women, you know; I'm against it."

He fingered the thin leather belt at his waist.

"If you get into trouble, send the boy back here or on to the valley on the pony. And—er—good luck with your work. Different people in the valley, you know—not all Christians—unreliable; wildish, too, as Koschade will tell you. Things were a bit sticky for him Christmas Day. Spears, you know; took off their clothes.

"There was something else I was going to mention to you—now what was it? Oh yes! Get Mrs. Koschade to cook you some of her coffee. Wonderful stuff. She's American, you know."

We made our farewells, mounted the camels, and lurched up the sandy bank of the Finke. For the first few miles we followed the meandering course of the river. Kinchika rode ahead on the pony while Tjalkalieri walked, pulling the two camels behind him. Soon he joined Kinchika. The camels plodded along slowly despite my "giddaps" and whipping. A racing camel can travel considerable distances in good time, but ones loaded like ours, and in poor condition, could at best walk only three miles an hour; so there was plenty of time to watch the slowly passing landscape.

Constantly the camels paused to take in mouthfuls of saltbush. Often the rear pack camel, when it stopped to eat, had its head jerked suddenly as the riding camel pulled the rope between them taut. We had gone barely a mile when this happened. There was a bellow of pain from the "lady-in-waiting." The nose rope had jerked, torn her nose, and snapped. Deftly Tjalkalieri threw a rope round the camel's vicious mouth, holding it closed while he rethreaded the thin rope in the peg, talking softly the while in his own tongue to the enraged beast.

The breaking of the nose rope became a monotonously regular interruption to our progress. We had been on the track no more than two hours when there came another wild bellow from the pack camel. I looked back and saw its head flung in the air, its nose bloody. This time the animal's tender nose had been torn right through. The camel reared and turned, the boxes on either side swaying precariously and snapping the light boughs of the mulga as the animal plunged off the track. Its feet skidded on the loose pebbles to the side of the track, and it began to run.

Kinchika, several hundred yards ahead on the black pony, turned and began trotting back. Tjalkalieri accepted the situation with equanimity. "Good-by, camel," he said, waving his hand. "Good-by, Lady Who Waits." He laughed immoderately at his own joke.

I felt like yelling, "You damned fool! Get after it!" But there was something about Tjalkalieri's calm acceptance of the circumstances that indicated either a resignation which might well, for all I knew, be justified by the facts, or a confidence that the situation was thoroughly under control.

Kinchika flogged the pony into action and swept off into the mulga and desert oak. Lyn and I dismounted—I was glad of the respite from the unfamiliar swaying saddle and the chance to take a long draught from the canvas water bag —and turned to our friend.

"They'll be back by 'n by," he said, as he refused a mug of cool water. I noticed that he was perspiring.

I rolled a cigarette for myself and then one for Tjalkalieri. He enjoyed the luxury of an occasional smoke, but rolling a cigarette was an unfamiliar task to his fingers. We had noted that his chewing of pituri had become more frequent since our trip to the valley had been planned.

"Pituri grows in the valley," he said. "I will bring *lots* of it back with me." His arms described a huge circle and there was a sudden picture of camels loaded with masses of the precious plant. Almost certainly this was one of the private reasons our friend had welcomed the chance of visiting Areyonga: to replenish his own supplies and to indulge in some very profitable trading.

At Hermannsburg ten shillings (about one dollar) is paid for a small bag of the weed. This seems a small enough amount but, as an Aranda stockman receives but a quarter of this amount in actual cash each week (the rest of his wages are paid in rations), it is a bountiful reward for the collecting and drying of the weed.

When they can get it, the natives of the Center, even small children, chew pituri constantly. The plant (*Duboisia hopwoodii*) grows lush in Areyonga Valley but the hills around Hermannsburg have been denuded. It grows in bushes about three feet in height with clusters of white, moth-pollinated flowers. The leaves are spread on rocks to dry in the sun, and the crisp leaves are then crushed and mixed with the ash of an acacia (*Acacia salicinica*). When moistened in the mouth the alkaloid piturine is liberated. This is much the same in action as nicotine. It has been called "blackfellows' tobacco," but it is not smoked.

Sometimes pituri leaves are used to catch small game. Water holes are infused with the stuff. The animals become stupefied after drinking and their capture is relatively easy.

We had wondered if pituri were used during certain native ceremonies when the participants undergo painful ordeals: the cutting of cicatrices, burning of weals, tooth evulsion, pulling out of fingernails, circumcision and subincision. Novices, lads no older than Kinchika, who was alone now in the bush chasing a frightened camel, must suffer and show no signs of pain. Was pituri used to ameliorate their suffering? Wherever we asked, the answer was an emphatic "No!" But the hint was given that a sort of hypnotic trance is induced, either by the doctors or the postulants themselves, and that the successful cultivation of this art is a requirement for initiation. As further stages of "post-graduate" revelation of the secret life of the aborigines are undertaken by those who, for example, may aspire to be doctors or who have been chosen, more profound trance states are expected.

The three of us sat in the shade of a stunted gum tree. With the recent rains the eucalypti had suddenly blossomed, and the still air was heavy with the scent of their flowers. The small, black, stingless wild bees were active, and Tjalka-lieri watched them idly as if contemplating a raid on their nest.

But suddenly his eyes were drawn to the ragged, blue horizon, with a look of intensity we had not seen before. He looked swiftly in the direction the lad had taken in chasing the camel and again back to the distant range. I could see nothing unusual.

"Smoke," said Tjalkalieri.

Automatically I reached again for my tobacco pouch to roll a cigarette for him, but then I realized what he had seen.

"Smoke," he repeated. "The smoke of someone from Haast Bluff. If the boy gets back soon, we meet him at Lililtja."

"I can't see the smoke."

"It is there."

"How do you know it is the smoke of someone from Haast Bluff? Why not Areyonga?"

"I know. You will see."

"Do you know who is making the smoke?"

"No."

Lyn and I were immediately reminded of the vexing problem of the smoke signals of aborigines, about which so much has been written and so little is known. But was this a signal in the usual meaning of the term?

"Is the man sending a message to you?"

"No, it is his camp."

"How can you know this when all you can see is smoke?"

"There is something that tells me these things. You would not understand."

As we looked toward the ranges, my wife and I could now just discern the faint, straight, vertical line of smoke.

"I have heard," I said, "that the message is in the smoke—there are little things you see in the smoke. And when you make smoke to send a message, you put your message into the smoke, so that even a white man who could see the signs in the smoke would be able to read the message."

"No, it is not in the smoke."

The answer was emphatic and I did not expect further elucidation.

Then Lyn spoke. "Tjalkalieri, when you see smoke, what does it do to you? Does it make you think?"

Suddenly I saw that she had perhaps reached the core of the problem.

"It makes me think, but I do not think. There is a great feeling rises up in me——" He broke off as though there were no words he could find in his own tongue or ours to convey his idea. But again I was surprised to find that penetrating understanding and choice of colorful expression that made Tjalkalieri such a valuable informant.

"It is," he said, "like wind from the head."

"Yes, we call it telepathy; but we don't know very much about it. Sometimes I wonder if we can be sure that it exists. And that, indeed, is why we have come to you people who seem to know so much of these things."

I am not sure that Tjalkalieri fully understood me; but he continued his explanation.

"When we see smoke we think, and often we find clearness like the cool springs of Lililtja, but at other times the mind is clouded and muddy. That is for men like Maleiaba and me—but a doctor knows, a doctor always knows."

"You saw this native's smoke and you knew it was not only his camp fire, but that he came from Haast Bluff. Now, if you wanted to send a special message by smoke how would you do it?"

"I would make the smoke so that the man could see it—a good big fire with green boughs that makes good smoke. When he sees it, he knows it is not a camp fire and he gets to thinking. And I am thinking, too, so that he thinks my thoughts."

Here, then, was one native's explanation of the mystery of smoke signals. The belief was clear, beautifully, forcefully clear. It was as clear a belief in telepathy as could be found. But what were the facts to justify it? That was one of the things our investigation was to probe.

Much, indeed, has been written about smoke signals. Many of the accounts suggest that there is nothing very extraordinary about smoke signals, that what little there is to be explained can be explained in terms of the native's unusually complete knowledge of what is going on about him, the movements of groups of natives close to his camp, and by inference. Other accounts lay emphasis on the large amount of detailed information apparently conveyed by smoke signal and declare that this could not possibly have been in the smoke itself. These accounts sometimes suggest imposture, gross exaggeration of the facts, or else leave the whole question unanswered. Evidence that some unusual perceptive capacity by the aborigines exists would tend to confirm the aboriginal statement of what occurs.

"Well, we'll see if you're right about this man—if the boy returns with the camel," I said, getting to my feet. As I did, I heard a faint *"Yokai"* and Kinchika could be seen in the distance on his black pony leading a now docile, and tired, camel along the track.

The incident had cost us more than an hour, and Lyn and I were anxious to push on to a water hole before nightfall. We had planned to reach Lililtja by late afternoon, and there was still about five hours' travel ahead of us.

Tjalkalieri tied the thin cord attached to the camel rope directly to a torn flap of the camel's nose (the peg had been lost) and we pushed on in silence.

The midday heat was oppressive and overpowering. Stunted saltbush and eucalypti were becoming thicker, and due to the recent rains there were occasional patches of heavier growth and gentle flowering shrubs where there was usually only bare red earth. Once or twice our slowly meandering party passed through tiny groves of green. We moved farther and farther away from the course of the Finke. Now and then we saw recent tracks of dingoes and perentie, giant desert lizard sometimes six feet long, and the winding furrows in sand or dust of the countless snakes that seemed to thrive in the area. Once Kinchika gave an exultant cry and galloped across to a low eucalyptus at the bottom of which we saw an untidy heap of bird feathers. This, we learned, was a sign that a carpet snake had caught a bird there and, sure enough, a moment or two later Kinchika galloped back with the still squirming body of a seven-foot snake draped across his pony's neck. The natives would eat well tonight.

The sun was low and the distant range stood out in deep relief when we reached Lililtja. The water was, as Tjalkalieri had said, crystal clear. It was running in a series of rock pools, shaded by cool gums and with lush grass on the banks.

"Wooshta—woosh, woosh!" The camels were made to kneel and the boxes and saddle were lifted off. Kinchika took the animals downstream to water them and hobbled them for the night.

We ate a hearty meal. Tjalkalieri cooked the snake on glowing coals for himself and the boy, and Lyn and I had sardines on bread made at Hermannsburg by one of the missioners, with some tomatoes from the mission garden. We had barely finished when a smile split Tjalkalieri's face. With an I-told-you-so look he pointed at the track and murmured, "Cuttacora." How he knew who the native was at that moment I do not know.

A moment or two later we saw him, a short but solidly built native striding along with two or three spears and a *woomera* in his hands. Some hundreds of yards behind him came a short-haired woman we presumed to be his wife. On her back, in a string bag, was a tiny, naked aboriginal child. In one hand the woman held a bundle of miscellaneous possessions tied in a large colored cloth, and clinging to the other hand was a flaxen-haired girl of about six. Behind her came a boy a little younger than Kinchika, carrying a large crossbred cattle dog in his arms. Another dog followed at his heels.

The spectacle was an object lesson in the aborigines' struggle for survival in this unfriendly environment. The hunters—the man and his dogs—must always be fresh, ready

to kill or capture the little game that there is in the area, so
that the women and children carry the burden.

Cuttacora and Tjalkalieri greeted each other warmly.

"You come from good country, I think," laughed Cuttacora, stroking Tjalkalieri's beard. "The grass grows on your
face. Tell me of the people at Hermannsburg; I long to see
their faces. And the Aranda dogs, do they still play their
games with the little colored stones?" He imitated a game of
marbles. We were to notice later, in the valley, how merci-
lessly the vigorous tribal Pitjendadjara lampooned the miserable and degraded Aranda; and we wondered how long it
would be before the exalted superiority of the Pitjendadjara
would wither with the encroachment of the white man.

While the woman sat at a distance, the men talked with
noisy merriment. "Tell me of our brother Maleiaba, you man
with many women," chuckled Cuttacora, chewing at a piece
of the cooked snake that the camel man had given him. "Is
he as fat still as the moon? And is his head as hairless?"

"And you tell me," said Tjalkalieri, after giving a brief account of the bone-pointing play that he and the little Ayers
Rock man had performed for me in the spinifex, "you tell
me of Pitamundri, the man with three fingers. He has traveled much in these hot days on his scraggy camel and prom-
ised to tell of great things in the south near Ernabella."

"These things have been told at the great *corroboree* at
Haast Bluff. Then the people said there was an empty place
where Tjalkalieri should stand. Some have gone to the valley.
I lead those who return to Hermannsburg, for my woman has
been ill and that old clever-fellow, Winjin, said she must leave
or else die, for the spirits are not strong about her where the
hills are high and the nights cold."

The men continued their talking. Cuttacora's boy had
joined Kinchika at a downstream rock pool and the two of
them were threshing the water with whips of fencing wire.
The concussion brought tiny fish to the surface, and these

they had gathered on a rock near them. After a time the lads brought their catch to the camp fire. They held the fish by the tails over the embers for a moment or two and then consumed them—head, guts, bones, and all.

As the Central Australian night settled over us and Lyn began to prepare our simple beds—the canvas used on the camel saddles—I walked over to the two men and asked Cuttacora if he would make camp with us overnight.

"The moon is full and we walk in the cool time, for we rested in the day," he said. We clasped hands. "When you return to Hermannsburg you will find me—me and my one woman!" Tjalkalieri squirmed and they both laughed.

The man picked up his spears and began to walk along the track we had come. The woman and children rose and walked after him. Before they disappeared in the gloom, I noticed that both dogs were now walking and Cuttacora had taken the boy onto his back and was carrying the girl in his arms. He said something to his wife, and his clear laughter rang through the night.

As the moon rose, clear and full, the four of us sat around our fire. Tjalkalieri was quiet and I wondered if something were troubling him. I asked him. He looked at Lyn and, placing his arm around Kinchika's shoulders, he said, "The boy has told me——" He paused and began again. "There is much that we dark people do not know; much we must learn from you——"

"Yes?"

"Tonight the boy saw you, after you had eaten, go to the water. There you took something, and as you touched it a little white thing that moved like a snake came out. You made it lie on a stick you took from a bag, and you put it to your mouth. Your mouth became frothy like a bull that is angry, and when you spat into the water it became cloudy. The boy would like to know of this strange thing."

Lyn and I realized that this must have been the first time

that these two natives had seen teeth cleaned western fashion. We laughed aloud and were immediately ashamed to have embarrassed our companions.

The incident was not without value. It showed something of the native's closeness of observation of something quite unfamiliar. It, and other such incidents, gave us a frame of reference of a sort by which we could evaluate the native description of things with which *we* were unfamiliar.

Tjalkalieri stoked the fire bright, and we turned in for the night. He and Kinchika disappeared beneath a blanket. As I lay there looking at the stars, a dingo howled nearby. I walked across to our baggage and took out my rifle. Soon I fell asleep, but I dozed lightly and a dingo howled again. I opened my eyes and saw it in the light of the moon on the far side of the Lililtja waters. As I grasped my rifle, I noticed Kinchika sliding along on his belly toward the animal, dragging a spear beside him. He seemed to glide along like a shadow, noiselessly.

"Come back, boy!" Tjalkalieri's voice broke the silence. "It's a mummy dingo."

Bashfully the boy stood up and walked back to the camp. I heard the native explain carefully to him in muffled tones that the one pound (two dollars) bonus obtained for the scalp of a "mummy dingo" was poorly earned money, for "mummy dingoes" produced many more bonus-earning baby dingoes, and should never be killed except in self-defense.

The air was crisp when we loaded the camels the following morning. For most of the morning I walked along the track ahead of the camels, but as the day wore on and the vast cone that was Mount Warber loomed closer and closer, we encountered patches of loose sand and spinifex that became more frequent, and I rode again. Red, rocky crags, bare and grotesque, rose on our left, the foothills of the Krichauff Range.

At the base of Mount Warber Kinchika followed fresh

dingo tracks, and the two natives, who were to return by themselves, agreed to leave the hunt for them to the return trip. Our next stop was at Gilbert Springs, a water hole covered by logs and near which we found date palms that had been planted by the anthropologist Sir Baldwin Spencer half a century before. The water from the springs was thick with green algae, but it was drinkable and, in any case, was the last permanent water hole before reaching the valley.

There was no track after leaving Gilbert Springs—just bare spinifex-studded sand—and I was forced to ride the camel again. The little black pony was slowed to a heavy, plodding walk. There were skeletons of cattle and marsupials, bare and white in the crimson sands. Far on the right horizon Mount Sonder, blue and serene, stood out from the range. The heat was oppressive, parching, and the hours passed slowly. The heat became too much for Lyn, and I feared that she might fall from the camel, so we rested a short time in the mean shade of one of the few stunted gums we occasionally came across growing in little clusters. We bathed our heads with handkerchiefs soaked in the precious water. The natives would not drink; they sternly held to a self-imposed discipline to drink infrequently, if at all, during the day. Tjalkalieri took Lyn's place on the camel, and she and the boy rode on the little mare.

Once we came across some recent camel tracks. Tjalkalieri looked at them carefully. "They belong to Wilfred's camel. He was racing it."

We had heard that Wilfred, a handy man at Areyonga, had called at Hermannsburg a little while before to get a new battery for the radio and collect the mail that had accumulated there for the Areyonga missionary.

"It was getting dark and the camel went lame."

So the messages that the desert sands hold are read—by those who can read them.

The Krichauff Ranges rose forbiddingly on our left. As

the hours passed Kinchika looked more and more anxiously at the ragged pattern of peaks stretching endlessly into the distance, watching for the break he knew would lead us over the mountains.

Then, on one of the frequent stops to drink we discovered that a water bag, rubbing against the camel box, had sprung a leak and was empty.

"How far to Areyonga?" I asked the natives. Distance means little to aborigines. Tjalkalieri replied, "Maybe seven miles, maybe seventy. I don't know." We had to smile.

As the sun sank low and I was beginning to wonder if we had better make a dash back to Gilbert Springs, Kinchika gave a cry and urged his pony on. Yes, he could see the "pointer," he said, miles in the distance yet, where we would turn into the range and begin to climb.

Two hours later we started the climb. The brush, mulga and desert oak, became thicker and the camels had to force their way along the path indicated by the boy, snapping off light boughs, the boxes on their backs swaying dangerously. A thick twig pierced one camel's side and there were redder patches in the red sand.

The pebbles beneath the camels' feet gave insecure footing. We reached a clear patch, a half-mile or more of steep ascent over boulders and pebbles rich red in color, magnificent to see as the sun cast its last light over them. This was a feature that we felt should be named. "Devil's Marbles" immediately came to mind, but the name had already been used for a strange rock formation near Alice Springs. Tjalkalieri suggested "Aranda Marbles." We laughed at his contemptuous reference to the game played by the men at Hermannsburg, and the red, rocky patch went unnamed.

We all walked. As we began the ascent, there was a cry of warning from Kinchika, now leading his pony and bringing up the rear. I looked round in time to see the camel boxes tilted dangerously and spilling their contents on the ground.

The bellyband had snapped. More time to be wasted; it was getting dark and we had no water. Tjalkalieri and I took off our leather belts and made a makeshift bellyband with them. But the real problem was to load the camel again, as camels will not kneel on rocky ground. In darkness we tried to force the beast down so that the boxes could be hitched on again, but without success.

We decided to abandon all our gear except a torch, a billy-can, and some food. I packed my cameras as best I could and hoped I would be able to recover them later. The climb was resumed by torchlight; we dragged the unwilling camels behind us. Soon we came across a more or less well-defined track with stone markers to point the way. Lyn and I felt our thirst to be unbearable, but the natives did not complain. Occasionally Kinchika sang fragments of a native song.

The summit was reached and we had to follow our barely discernible track along ridges that were, we found later, sometimes half a mile, sometimes only fifty yards, across. But the track seemed endless. Water was becoming a serious need. On these heights there was no hope of finding a soak, only unreliable casual water, and wherever the beam of the torch searched was bare and dry. We sat down to rest; the rocks were still hot. Lyn cried out as a snake she had disturbed slithered nearby.

Somewhere in these ranges Albert Namatjira, the famous aboriginal artist, had discovered copper ore. The region had not been accurately surveyed (as we knew too well) and it was not known if Albert's discovery was on the aboriginal reserve, mission property, or the outskirts of a cattle station. So the copper was still unmined, and Albert is still painting pictures. His paintings bring him an income double that of the average professional man in Australia.

We had, for the moment, lost interest in the beauty of the country, and its mineral resources. Tjalkalieri wanted to make camp for the night.

About half a mile farther on we found water. My torch caught a reflection from the depths of a gully. Tjalkalieri climbed down and brought back a billycan full. Water! We gulped huge mouthfuls, poured it over ourselves. Then we suddenly remembered the natives standing silently by and offered a mugful to Kinchika and Tjalkalieri. Stoically they refused it, said they would wait till we reached the valley.

A short while later the track became more clearly defined, and soon we were making an obviously steep descent. The track zigzagged back and forth across the mountainside. The moon had risen, but we were in the shadows and had only the light of the torch. Sometimes the track was a mere three feet wide; on one side was a bare rock face, on the other a sheer drop of almost a thousand feet. No one who knew the track, and who was in his right senses we decided later, would have attempted a night descent. It was not surprising that our camel man had wanted to camp at the top overnight.

Once or twice the camel packs slipped—the makeshift bellyband was not a complete success—and Tjalkalieri and I balanced precariously on the brink to push them back on again.

Soon we could make out the lights of tiny camp fires, and the ghostly sound of natives' voices echoed up the walls of the valley to us. We could hear music, too; a raucous phonograph played "Good-night, Irene."

As the track became easier Kinchika rode ahead—the little pony was still lively—and after a while we could hear the voices below us become more excited. Some of the lights brightened and began to move. A few natives bearing flaming torches came up the track to meet us.

Tjalkalieri's friends threw their arms about him. Some of the natives took the camels, and we were guided to quarters for the night.

Early in the morning the missionary, Mr. V. Koschade, and his wife came to greet us.

"Your boy Tiger is taking some men and fresh camels to recover your gear," said the missionary. The Hermannsburg pastor's comment about unreliable natives came to mind.

"I thought you might like something to refresh you," smiled the missioner's wife. She had brought some food, including a huge, ripe watermelon, and in her hand she held a large billy full of steaming black coffee.

▌▌▌▊▌▌▌▊▌▌▌▌▊▌▌▌▌▊▌▌▐▌▌▌▊▌▌▌▊▌▌▌▊▌▌▌▌▌▌▊▌▌▌▌▌▌▌▊▌▌▌▊▌▌▌▌▌▊▌▌▌▌▌▌▌▌▊▌▌▌▌▌▊▌▌▌▌▌▌▌▌

CHAPTER 4

A Witch Doctor's Ways

For generations the Areyonga Valley has been a favorite meeting place of aboriginal tribes. It is forty miles in length and runs east and west. At the western end is Palm Valley. Both entrances to the valley have permanent water, and when any rain falls a creek runs the entire length— at least for a few days. Formerly the valley belonged to the western group of the Aranda, sometimes called the Loritja, but the members of that tribe who now survive are centered about Hermannsburg, and the Pitjendadjara people from the Petermann Ranges have moved in.

Their sacred *churingas,* age-old tribal objects, often ornately carved, they have brought with them. But the *corroborees* associated with many of them can never be performed again as cattle stations cover some of the sacred grounds. (A *corroboree* is an aboriginal ceremony, sometimes sacred, in other instances profane. The word itself is thought to have originated on the east coast but is now in common use in all aboriginal tribes.)

We found that the Areyonga missionary had created a marvelously productive garden there. He had installed a simple system of irrigation, and watermelons, rock melons, tomatoes, carrots, and onions grew to perfection. This very valley was included by Dr. J. Bradfield (designer of the Sydney

Harbour Bridge) in a plan for the irrigation of Central Australia and western Queensland.

The mission buildings lie on the floor of the valley and the red-rock walls rise almost perpendicularly on each side, barely a couple of hundred yards apart. Ordinary speech echoes from the walls, and loud noises reverberate through the valley. The rock formation is soft, and there are bright-red scars where rocks have recently slipped from the face. Lyn and I noticed goats grazing around the tiny settlement. The herd, now tended solely by the natives, provides milk and meat, a welcome change in our diet while we were there. During the heat of the day we were amused to notice goats, in search of shade, resting in the *wurlies* (small grass huts) of the natives. No one seemed to mind.

Until Tjalkalieri returned there was little work we could do with the natives, for few of them spoke any English and our knowledge of Pitjendadjara was of the most elementary sort. When he did return that evening, with every item of our baggage safe and carefully packed, he had a long conference with a number of the elders. Later he told me that he had explained to them something of the nature of our investigations and the tests we used, which he had seen, and they had agreed to lend their assistance.

Most impressive of these men was Winjin, a clever-man of wide repute. At times his eyes held a look of gentle melancholy; at other times they could pierce with a look of terrifying fierceness. Winjin was of early middle age (though he was referred to by other natives as an "old fellow"), very active and muscular; his carriage was erect and presence always dignified. But there was nothing, apart from an aloofness of manner, to distinguish him from other natives. He had no badge of office, so to speak, no authenticating mark; his office had no special tribal privileges. He was respected by all tribal members, however, and when he spoke his pronouncements had an air of finality about them.

He spoke infrequently. Indeed, on my first meeting with him he spoke but two words. Lyn and I were examining a number of aboriginal artifacts we had collected during our stay in the Center—spearheads and miscellaneous stone tools. I held in my hand one neat, symmetrical spearhead I had found, along with a number of broken and discarded pieces, in a quarry that had probably been worked by aboriginal craftsmen for centuries.

Aloud I said, "I wonder why this one was thrown away."

Winjin glanced at me with a look that could have been of scorn and said, "Too light." Then he gathered his flaxen-haired, eighteen-month-old son in his arms and walked away.

Dr. Ronald Berndt, an experienced field anthropologist, has recorded this impression of clever-men. "Informants stressed that 'you could always tell a clever man no matter where you saw him'; the distinction from other men was not physical, but could be observed by the 'intelligent' light in his eyes which differed inexplicably from that of other men. Further, great doctors were said to be enveloped in a peculiar atmosphere which caused ordinary people to feel diffident in their presence."

Some clever-men carry a few magical articles about with them, perhaps entwined in the beard, but usually there is nothing to distinguish the doctor from other tribal members. The clever-man is, as far as we are able to gather, pleasant in his social relations; he may marry, fall ill, or suffer as a result of malignant magic.

He freely uses conjuring tricks and miscellaneous deceits in the practice of his magic, particularly in healing. This aspect caused the German missionary Strehlow, who worked in Central Australia, and others who have had close association with aborigines, to claim that clever-men are charlatans and impostors. It is clear, however, that the average clever-man has a basically sound, if rather colored, knowledge of the psychiatric practices he employs.

Within his own culture he is a person of special knowledge, initiative, and self-assurance. Whether or not he possesses genuine psychical abilities (Winjin gave no evidence of this in the tests we gave him), there is no question that he is of unusual mental stature.

The clever-man is a keen observer, both of nature and of men. He maintains a watchful eye on the behavior of tribal members, particularly if it may be inimical to the welfare of the tribe as a group. He is unobtrusive, but he is the supreme arbiter. He need not be, but often is, one of the tribal elders—the council which loosely governs the tribe's activities—and when he is, he is usually the dominating personality in the group. His sphere of influence is comprehensive; his administration of it both vigorous and subtle.

Often a tribe has a number of clever-men or doctors and they usually work in harmony. Sometimes, however, differences between them occur. These may be settled amicably, or by a competitive display of magic—the doctor producing the greatest number of magic cords or the widest and most spectacular range of magical feats being held to have established his ascendancy—or the dispute may develop into savage sorcery.

Most aboriginal doctors cover the whole range of magic, but there is a tendency to specialization, so that one may be renowned as a rain maker, another as a healer, and so on. The doctor is the tribal protector. He reads and interprets the signs of nature, makes rain or aids hunting parties with his magic. He protects the tribe, too, against neighboring tribes; this he is able to do, he says, with his magical knowledge of what is going on in the surrounding country, for he takes psychical excursions or sends spirit familiars, usually totemic animals, to acquire the information for him. But often he has to needle, agitate, and stimulate the tribe to get them to do the things he wants them to do.

In aboriginal society, unlike other native groups, the queer, the feeble-minded, and the epileptic are not revered, nor do they have high offices of magic thrust upon them. In fact, abnormal states are rarely observed among tribal aborigines; it is unlikely that grossly abnormal natives are allowed to survive. The emphasis is on normality in this respect, but deep states of contemplation, merging into trance, are highly regarded.

There are, too, some clever-men about whom little is known. They lead lives of deep contemplation, are ascetics even by aboriginal standards, and rarely take part in tribal activities. They are celibates and mystics.

By sheer accident I won the regard of Winjin. Tjalkalieri told me that Winjin had passed by our quarters on the first night we were in the valley and had heard me snoring. As it is a native belief in this area, and some others, that when a person snores his soul has left the body on a psychical excursion, I had certain magical powers attributed to me!

Winjin's prestige was at its height when Lyn and I were in Areyonga Valley, for he was, among other things, a rain maker. And had not the area had its greatest rains for many, many years?

Rain making is, as might be expected, an important magical function in the case of the desert natives. In this area there are but two seasons—the dry, which extends over the greater part of the year, and the wet. Following the wet, which usually lasts for only a short time (in some years it may not occur at all) a transformation of the landscape takes place. The desert blooms. The sterile waste becomes bright with flowering plants, and animal life appears in a way that must seem to the aborigines a bountiful response to their magic.

The magical beliefs of the aborigines on rain making are beautifully simple: rain cannot occur unless the appropriate ceremonies are performed by them. So close is the self-world relationship that they consider the rain to be as dependent on them as they are on it.

Highly symbolic ceremonies must be carried out, but it needs the magical powers of the rain maker to produce the rain. In the center of the continent the ceremonies are of a seasonal nature, and usually the doctor will not attempt to make rain out of season. In some tribes the office of rain maker, unlike other magical offices, is hereditary.

On the coast the rain maker is called on for a more or less constant control of the weather—to make a storm to confound an enemy tribe or to break up a storm that enemy doctors have created to harm his people.

Lyn and I had discussed these strange powers with de-tribalized natives at Woodenbong, in northern New South Wales.

"When I was a little girl," said one of them, Rene Robinson, an old Gidabul woman, "I saw one of these old fellas make a storm at Casino. He was that old Mumbi's father." Mumbi is a native now living at Tabulam (N.S.W.).

"Well, missus," she said, as Lyn questioned her, "to do this clever thing he had to take his clothes off, proper-naked-fella-like. He was pretty wild with some other fellas, he was, missus, and I was pretty scared when I watched him. He stood there without any clothes on, and the sky was clean, without any clouds. He sang the song and a wind came up and blew about him. He talked to the wind—those old fellas could do that, you know—and told it to bring some storm clouds.

"Wasn't long before them clouds came, either. Big, black fierce clouds with thunder and lightning. I remembers seeing this old fella there making the storm to send away and hurt these other peoples; yes, I remembers it like it was yesterday."

At Woodenbong, too, we had been told about the old-time, storm-making powers of clever-men by an old man who himself was reputed to be clever.

"Yes," Danny Sambo had said as he sucked an old pipe from which the stem had been broken, "I seen them old fellows make storms. They could travel with the storms, too. My old grandfather used to do that. I seen him once when I was only a kid, and I nearly got killed for it."

"Was it a clear day?" I asked.

"Oh, yes, boss, so help me, it was clear until this old grandad of mine started to sing the storm song. Then the clouds started to come up and my father covered up my face with his waistcoat. There was so much thunder about I shivered with frights. But I sneaked a look and, so help me, there was the old fellow waving his arms about, singing his song, and the storm was getting fiercer and stronger. There was another old doctor fellow with my grandad, and he saw me looking, and they were both pretty angry. They were so angry, so help me, they broke up the storm right then and made it go away so I wouldn't see no more."

Danny Sambo grinned and showed toothless gums clenched on his pipe. "I was lucky they didn't kill me, wasn't I? Later on, when I had gone through the ring [been initiated] I saw them same old fellows break up a storm. It was at Kilcoy in Queensland. We could all see a terrible storm coming straight towards the town and everyone was frightened. Well, them old fellows took off their clothes and sang a song to the storm. It got closer and closer and then, so help me, it split into two parts. One part of it went to one side of the town and the other went to the other side. Them white peoples that knew about it were pretty glad my grandad and the other old fellow saved the town."

My wife and I try not to look skeptical when such accounts are given us by natives. I don't know if on this occasion our expression had betrayed us, but Danny Sambo hastened to say, "You needn't take my word for it. So help me, there was an old clever-fellow name of Jimmy McQuiltie could break storms, down Lismore way. You can ask Walter Page about him."

We asked Walter Page. Walter is a well-informed, intelligent native who has represented his people on the Aborigines Welfare Board of New South Wales. In his quiet, well-modulated voice Walter confirmed the account of the power of Jimmy McQuiltie to break up storms. "I have never seen it myself, Mr. Rose," he said, "but my mother told me many times about Jimmy McQuiltie. She and many others believe that he saved Lismore [N.S.W.] in 1910. There was a very violent storm. Trees were being uprooted, and as the storm reached the outskirts of the town, some houses had their roofs torn off. The people, that is the dark people, of course, appealed to McQuiltie. He took off his clothes, so that his power could flow freely from him, and he spoke to the storm. As if by a miracle, my mother told me, the storm divided and passed on either side of the town. She firmly believed that Jimmy McQuiltie saved Lismore."

"And what do you think, Walter?" We were anxious to have his opinion. He said he believed that in former times when his people, the Bundulung, were living in the tribal state, the doctors did indeed have the power to make or to break up storms. He thought that a power flowed from them, and they were able to mold natural events to their will or desire. He doubted the ability of any man living now to do this, however.

Another Woodenbong resident, Tom Kenny, said that he had personally seen clever-men sing the special storm songs and make storms. Then the doctors had disappeared, and he had later seen them actually in the storm clouds, directing the storm!

"Yes, I saw them all right. Right up in the clouds they were, taking the storm to enemy people."

"You could see their bodies?"

"Oh, yes! They were in the storms, flying about in it. I saw them with my own eyes. They did it with their magic cords."

Such were the beliefs we had found among the detribalized people on the coast; such were some of the fabulous eyewitness accounts we had recorded.

And it was with these accounts in mind that I questioned Tjalkalieri, and through him Winjin and other natives, at Areyonga. Five of us were seated in the evening near a huge rock and cave about half a mile from the tiny settlement. There was Tjalkalieri chewing pituri happily, with a spare wad behind each ear, elated in his role of interpreter; there was Winjin, quiet, reserved, thoughtful, perhaps impressed that my soul could, he thought, travel in the night; there was Tamelei, a tremendously big aboriginal (he was about six feet six inches tall) with a delicate aquiline nose; and there was an old man, whose name I never learned, who sat silently and nodded his head slowly as the others spoke. The soft glow of a camp fire lit their features.

"Tjalkalieri," I said, "I want Winjin to tell me how he made the great rains that have just finished."

I followed Tjalkalieri's interpretation of my question as best my knowledge of Pitjendadjara would allow me.

"He wants to know how you brought the great rains that have made the grasses shoot forth, given blossoms for the bees to make their honey, and fattened the kangaroos and euros, so that your people in the valley walk with full bellies and happiness swells in their hearts."

There was poetry in this native.

After a short discussion Winjin left the group. In a little while he returned, sat down, and solemnly placed in the center of the group a small, faintly carved piece of pearl shell. It was much smaller than its probable original size, and from its smoothness and shallowness of the carvings I presumed this was from age and constant handling. Tjalkalieri said this *churinga* had in it the "spirit of water." It had come from the "great water" that none of them had seen.

Such articles do travel, by fairly well-defined trade routes, from the natives on the northern coast of the continent a thousand or more miles into the interior. Ceremonies similarly pass down the trade routes.

Tjalkalieri explained that the clever-man, in this case Winjin, was able, by means of a special song (which he would not sing, for no more rain was desired just now!) to release the spirit of the water in the shell. In the ceremony, which he would not initiate until he was inspired so to do, he would spit upon the shell and whirl it through the air so that fine droplets, representing rain, fell on the old men who danced the rain dance about him.

Waiting for inspiration to go ahead with rain-making ceremonies is, in this area, probably little more than closely observing the seasons and noting such signs of nature as atmospheric conditions and the movements of ants that would indicate the imminence of rain. In the Herbert River area the supernatural being, *Kohin,* is asked by the natives to send rain only after they have heard frogs croaking for it.

Thus it is that, in the vast center of the continent, the rain *corroborees* are only held at certain times of the year, when there is a distinct prospect of rain; so it may be said that, in general, rain falls following the ceremonies. This type of rain making is an interesting example of the confusion between cause and effect that is superstitious thinking.

There have been occasions, it is true, when white men have induced natives to perform rain ceremonies out of season and rain has followed. Some of the accounts are, perhaps, a little too naïve; they certainly present no conclusive evidence of unusual powers on the part of the native rain makers.

Dr. A. W. Howitt, an early anthropologist, recorded an amusing incident that came to his notice. The event occurred in a time of severe drought. "[A rain maker] . . . and others of his tribe were camped at Morton's Plains, and on his boasting of his power to produce rain, the then owner of the station said to him: 'I will give you a bag of flour, some tea, and half a bullock, if you will fill my tank before tomorrow night.' The tank was a large excavation just finished. This was early in the morning and the rainmaker set to work at once, saying, 'All right, me make him plenty rain come.' The next day there was a tremendous thunderstorm, the rain fell over all the run, and the tank was filled." The native got his reward!

While the Pitjendadjara clever-man is singing his rain song and whirling the pearl shell, Tjalkalieri went on, translating Winjin's explanation as the other two natives nodded in agreement, younger initiates of the tribe have been powdering a whitish stone, probably gypsum, and sprinkling it onto small eucalyptus boughs they have broken off. At the appropriate time in the ceremony they approach the old man, making noises in imitation of thunder, and shaking the powder-laden boughs representing clouds over the older men, they produce a tolerable imitation of rain. This is the climax of the ceremony. The magic in this case was clearly imitative.

"The other tribes about here, do they have a *corroboree* like this?" I asked.

"I can tell of the Dieri," said Tamelei quietly, "for I have traveled much and know these people."

Before Tamelei went ahead with his account, however, the pearl shell that had been produced by Winjin was passed from one to the other in the group. Each man handled it reverently for a few moments and then passed it on. When it had returned to Winjin, he wrapped it carefully in a cloth dirtied by kangaroo fat and red ocher (thought to be a life-giving substance since it resembles blood) and returned it to its hiding place.

Tamelei gave his version of the Dieri ceremony, at first hesitantly, in his own tongue with an occasional English word. Tjalkalieri translated for me. Soon he warmed to the unfamiliar task of explanation and presented a vivid picture of an involved and lengthy magical ceremony, rich in symbolism, and a splendid example of the entire tribe and sometimes representatives from neighboring tribes co-operating in a magical activity.

As he spoke Tamelei illustrated his description with eloquent movements of his hands; the other natives leaned forward, absorbed, and the fire burned low. As I watched the quiet, intense faces of my companions, I felt something of the savage appeal of primitive magic; I sensed the utter dependence of these people on their ceremonies, their clever-men, and their attempt to influence the forces of nature.

The Dieri are a desert tribe who live to the south of the Aranda and Pitjendadjara. When the council of elders, in consultation with the rain makers, has decided that the seasonal ceremonies should be held, great activity takes place, accompanied by excitement and anticipation of the result.

First a large shallow hole is dug, and over it is built a conical hut of logs and boughs. The women of the tribe inspect the hut and the old men huddle inside it while the young men remain outside. Two or more rain makers have their arms pierced and, when they are bleeding freely, they spatter their blood on the men around. Down from white cockatoos is thrown into the air. It floats downward and some of it attaches itself to the sticky blood on the performers. The down represents clouds; the blood, rain.

While this is going on other men have powdered some white stones and now scatter the powder into the air over a water hole. This represents rain falling and filling the holes.

Following this, young men, with their heads down, charge the conical hut and butt it (here Tamelei slammed a clenched fist into his open palm) until they knock it down.

"Don't they hurt themselves?" I interrupted.

"Yes, but this they do for the rain to come; it is little enough."

The butting of the hut represents the piercing of clouds. When this is done, the whole tribe join together in addressing the spirits of the rain. Looking to the heavens, they call attention to the impoverished state of their country, the lack of plant and animal life, and their starving children. They are then content that they have done their part in the production of rain, which will, or should, follow in a few days.

I asked the men if storms were ever made to inflict harm on enemy tribes. This puzzled them for a while because the phenomenon seemed to them far removed from the productive magic of rain making. Then Winjin said, "Whirlie whirlie," and Tjalkalieri explained that clever-men could make whirlwinds in which they travel to distant places. All whirlwinds, he said, have a magical origin. "If you see one of these whirlie whirlies you can tell an old fellow has been at work."

And, after all these ceremonies, if too much rain falls? Winjin would make no comment, but some investigators have recorded that natives became "frenzied" and begged the spirits to exercise moderation.

Just after Tamelei finished his account, and I had thanked him for his clear and colorful description, we heard female voices raised in anger coming from the camp area. As we walked back, we saw in the moonlight a small group gathered around two women. One of the women had a long, thick digging stick which she wielded with two hands, hitting the other woman soundly over the head. She then passed the stick to the other woman who, after wiping some blood from her eyes, hit the first woman a resounding blow. So they continued, each in turn hitting the other, and so they would have gone on till one had collapsed if Winjin had not stepped out ahead of us and, with a few short, sharp words, broken up their quarrel.

As I was leaving Tjalkalieri for the night, I asked him what the two women had been fighting about.

"Men," said the man with two wives, grinning broadly. "Maybe me!" He moved into the shadows with a quiet laugh.

That evening Lyn and I discussed the evidence for rain making. I felt that we could safely ignore the few accounts given by white men which suggested that native doctors did in fact produce rain. Some of the accounts given us were amusing. Ronald Berndt, had told us of an occasion in Adelaide when, on a fine clear day, he had visited an old man disabled by infirmity to record some tribal songs. One of these was the rain song. The native demurred, saying that rain would follow. Berndt, however, scoffed at the idea and eventually persuaded the native to sing his song. Later that afternoon, when he left the hospital where the native was convalescing, Berndt was drenched to the skin by an unexpected shower!

It could have been a remarkable coincidence. The evidence based on such anecdotal accounts is flimsy; the phenomenon would be difficult enough to verify even if it did occur. Certainly it did not have the same weight as the evidence for sickness or death following bone pointing.

Then there were the accounts of the native peoples here in the desert. Clearly the ceremonies were seasonal ones, unconnected causally with their presumed effects. The clevermen followed the tradition or, perhaps in a few cases because of their superior knowledge of natural events, were guilty of sly opportunism.

Evidence given by the more or less sophisticated coastal people who claim to have seen the dramatic production of storms, the dispersal of storms, or clever-men actually in storm clouds was more puzzling. Only one native offered an explanation that seemed reasonable. He was Walter Green, a half-caste Woodenbong aboriginal who described a storm he had seen a clever-man make some years before. The doctor had done this, Green said, by putting an axhead in the ground and singing over it. When Green had asked how he performed the apparent miracle, the old man had told him he sent cold out from himself and precipitated the rain. "Often does rain when it gets cold," commented Walter.

The investigator can afford to neglect nothing; extraordinary, perhaps meaningful, beliefs and practices tumble before him, demanding explanation. Our informants had, in general, been reliable; on other matters where we could check them their information was sound. How could they give such apparently fanciful accounts with such obvious sincerity? Let us speculate: A clever-man might say, "You saw the way that storm split. I did that." Of such stuff are legends made. With the passage of time the remembrance of what was seen had perhaps been embellished and modified to fit in with a traditional pattern of belief. Fraud, delusion, coincidence, hypnotism—and overlying all these possibilities was the undoubted prestige impact of the clever-men on their somewhat credulous public. Was it possible that the doctors could, in fact, exercise a sort of "mind force"? Our tests would throw some light on this aspect, we felt. And if they didn't, the psychology of evidence, the effects of suggestion, the production of hallucinations, might.

In fact our dice tests were completely negative. We found not a scrap of experimental evidence to support the view that clever-men or anyone else could clearly influence the weather by a mind force alone.

Tjalkalieri began the next day with a joke on the previous day's discussions. He looked at the clear blue sky and remarked in an offhand way, "Huh, no one been singing!"

I had determined to spend the day questioning this man and his friends on other forms of productive magic. As we wandered through the camp, I noticed a burly native of the tribe who had fallen quickly into western ways. He was dressed colorfully, like an American cowboy, from his broad-brimmed sombrero to his spurred, high-heeled riding boots.

"That's Adolph," said Tjalkalieri. "The mission have given him cattles and each day he rides out to look after them."

I did not then notice the smirk on my friend's face, or understand his sarcasm. I was marveling at the uncharacteristic industry of an aboriginal. The mission, I learned, had tried to assist individual natives to establish themselves in the cattle industry. Adolph was one of a few who had been entrusted with a dozen or so head of "cattles" which were left to his entire personal supervision.

I watched the big native as his family fussed about him. Carefully he adjusted his clothing as he waited for a boy to bring up his horse. He examined the neatly coiled rope on one side of the saddle and the rifle on the other. Then he swung himself onto his horse, grasped a bottle of soft drink passed him by his wife, took a deep swig at it and, still holding it in his hand, spurred his horse's flanks and galloped off. His family's admiring gaze followed him till he disappeared around a bluff in a cloud of red dust.

Tjalkalieri and I followed slowly and were joined by the other men. We walked around the bluff of rock and to the mouth of a cavern overlooking a muddy water hole. This was what Lyn and I called the "men's club," a place women did not dare frequent. And there, unsaddling his horse, his bottle of soft drink on a rock beside him, was Adolph!

I looked at Tjalkalieri. "Adolph is looking after his cattles!" Tjalkalieri held his sides as laughter bubbled from him. "Tonight he will go back, tired, after his hard work!"

A grin had split Adolph's face and he walked across and spread himself comfortably on a rock near us. He chewed some pituri for a while, finished his bottle of soft drink; then, pulling his sombrero down over his face, he went to sleep.

I decided to open the discussion on productive magic by recounting some of the material Lyn and I had collected from Aranda informants at Hermannsburg. This was always sound policy in discussing magic; it gave the natives a clear picture of the type of information being sought, started their thoughts running on their own similar beliefs and practices, and was some evidence that other natives had vouchsafed that type of information to us.

Ceremonies similar to rain making are held by the Aranda in a kangaroo-increase ritual. Such ceremonies, designed to bring about the increase of animals and plants, are commonly found among native peoples. In the case of the aborigines the complex totemic organization is involved. Each totemic group is charged with the responsibility of ensuring the fecundity and plentifulness of the animal or plant it represents. The responsibility is a magical one and its proper discharge is sedulously followed.

"The kangaroo men of the Aranda people," I told the Pitjendadjara men, "come together at a secret stone and spill their blood on it so that the spirits of the kangaroos can be released from the rock and there will be many to hunt." I did not add that the ceremony is held with a good deal of zest when there is, as indicated by other aspects of nature, promise of a good season.

The old men nodded in agreement. Yes, they said, their people have the same sort of rituals, and so do the Dieri, and the Aluridja, the Kokata, the Wonggai, and the Ulapula. In almost all of them the men of the totem spill their blood so that their totem shall have increase. In some tribes the women take part to ensure plentiful supplies of honey or edible roots. They have their magical songs and swing their booming bull-roarers.

I asked about hunting magic. Winjin proudly said that hunting parties often came to him, before setting out, to have him treat their weapons. He explained, through Tjalkalieri, that by putting a boomerang or a spear to his mouth, a power passed from him into the weapon and helped it fly straight to its mark. The psychological aid to simple-thinking aborigines of such a procedure was obvious—unless their ability with spear or boomerang was so poor as to make them lose faith in the clever-man and the power he had put into the weapons. Winjin claimed, too, that his power was so great he could go out into the bush and, having seen, say, a kangaroo, he could fix his eye on it so that after a while it became "silly" and he was able to spear it with ease.

The old man whose name I did not know entered into friendly dispute with the clever-man. "Your skill with a spear is so great, your eye so keen, you do not need to stun the animals with the great force that is in you and makes you clever."

It was a skillfully put argument. If Winjin accepted the flattery about his normal hunting prowess, he minimized the greatness of his magic. But he countered gracefully. "My skill either with the spear or with the head [mind] I am willing to match with yours." The others applauded the cut and parry. I could see that the magic of the hunt was not as seriously regarded as other magic.

One important aspect of aboriginal productive magic is devoted to the increase and good health of the natives themselves, and the psychical origin of children is part of a mystical doctrine that permeates their beliefs.

An Aranda native had told me of the mysterious *ratappa* stone. When a woman visited this stone in company with her husband, she became pregnant. In a vision she often saw the spirit children about the stone; previous physical relations with her husband were merely a preparation for the child to enter her. In a simple ritual carried out at the stone the man ties his hair girdle around the stone and exhorts the spirit children to observe the attractiveness of his wife whom they had, apparently, previously ignored.

"I know the stone," said Tjalkalieri. "The Aranda say its power is very great. If a young woman who does not want a baby has to pass by the stone, she twists her face so that she looks old, she walks bent like an old woman and hobbles with a stick. As she goes by she says, 'Keep away from me. I am an old woman!'"

Sometimes a woman who does not wish to have a child conceives. Abortion of a rather primitive kind may follow. Aborigines are inordinately fond of their children. But they are obliged sometimes to restrict their numbers, and therefore abortions are procured or newborn infants are allowed to starve or are choked with fine dust. If a woman already encumbered with a small child were to have yet another, her food-gathering ability would be restricted and she would be unable to travel with the tribe on its wanderings. Moreover, the natives know just how many individuals their tribal country can normally support, and they restrict their population to just that level.

When children are retained (which they are in most cases), their mothers carry out magical rituals to enhance their growth, particularly the boys'. Muscular development, keenness of sight and hearing, and fluency of speech are carefully watched as the child grows.

The question of whether or not aborigines understand the paternal role in conception has been widely debated. The confusion has arisen, it would seem, because when anthropologists have asked their questions, they have been given ritual replies. A normal native informant, asked about bone pointing, for instance, tends to give a description of the ritual, something of the magical background perhaps, but rarely does he state the psychological principle, either of suggestion or a mind force, which he knows quite well. Similarly, the traditional answers have been given on childbirth. On the other hand skilled investigators have elicited information that has left them with no doubt that the significance of the sexual act was fully understood by tribal natives, even if the physiological knowledge of reproduction was of the most elementary sort.

In the case of Tjalkalieri, one of whose wives had a "halfcaste kid," there was little doubt that he clearly understood the role he played in reproduction. I doubt if he acquired the information from his contact with whites.

The day's discussion ended as usual on a hilarious note. The humor of the aborigines, who are so often portrayed as a sober, unimaginative race, seemed to me to be irrepressible.

It was, perhaps, part of their defense against an unfriendly environment.

I had been talking about a practice of the young men of the Aranda tribe who have not yet reached puberty. They are allowed access to the *churinga* (in this case a flat, sacred stone) of the Jerboa rat, a desert marsupial with extraordinarily long whiskers. They rub the *churinga* on their hairless faces to encourage the growth of whiskers. (In this case also, it may be noted, success follows the magical ceremony, though we know the two to be unrelated causally.)

As we were talking about this practice, Tjalkalieri began to laugh. He hid his face in his hands and his body convulsed. Between gusts of laughter he cried, "Maleiaba!" The other natives joined in the merriment. For a moment I did not understand.

"What about Maleiaba?"

"He hides his head under a shameful hat. Yet he could rub his baldness away with the Aranda stone!"

CHAPTER 5

Leech and Coroner

"Look out!" cried Tjalkalieri. "Snake!" There was a movement in the long grass and I saw an olive-green snake, its forked tongue flicking back and forth, slithering toward us. It was about six feet long, with a thick, bluntish head. There was nothing at hand with which to kill it—the stunted bushes in the valley provided no suitable stick.

"Is it poisonous?" I asked.

"Too —— right!" Tjalkalieri let forth a western expletive I had not previously heard him use. He took a small stone and threw it near the reptile. It stopped momentarily at the disturbance and Tjalkalieri called, "Come on. Run!"

After a somewhat undignified scramble over the rough ground for a hundred yards or so, we panted to a standstill. When we had got our breath back my friend said, "By golly, you run better than 'Lady Who Waits'!" I ignored his gentle sarcasm.

"What would you have done if you had been bitten?" I asked.

"See that old Winjin fellow," replied Tjalkalieri, without hesitation. Strangely, the incident fitted well with the subject matter of my talk that morning with him about the powers of clever-men to cure various ailments, and Tjalkalieri had just mentioned that Winjin was almost as renowned a healer as he was a rain maker.

He told me of some of the "normal" methods that Winjin used to treat a variety of ailments. Broken limbs, for example, were set by the doctor, enclosed in splints of stiff bark which were tightly tied and sometimes packed with mud or clay. If a native had a fever, the clever-man often steamed him above a small fire of masses of green eucalyptus foliage. In these types of illnesses there seemed to be little or no magic, although if a native believed, for example, that he had fallen from a tree because a bough had been made weak by some magical means, then counter magic would probably be employed by the doctor.

It seemed clear, however, that patently ordinary illnesses and accidents were treated with little mystical accompaniment.

"And what would Winjin do to treat snake bite?"

"I have seen him do this. Sometimes he hits the bitten place hard with a clever stone so that the badness stays there. Then he takes a sharp stone and cuts the flesh. He puts his mouth there and sucks out the badness and spits it out. With the blood and the badness he spits out the scales and the bones of the snake."

I was interested to note that, whereas a magical stone supposed to be in a patient's body would be removed without leaving a mark, the flesh was actually cut in the case of a snake bite.

"How do the scales and bones get into the person?"

"From the snake. The person has the badness of the snake in him."

Here was a clear example of the type of trickery employed by clever-men in effecting their cures, such deception as has led some investigators to call them charlatans and impostors. But the psychological effect of seeing objects, such as scales and bones, symbolizing the snake, removed from him is no doubt of value to a stricken native, and therefore, in this magical climate, well justified.

Other objects, usually of a magical nature, are "removed" from natives who are suffering from illnesses that are, perhaps, imaginary.

"Do many of your people call on Winjin to cure them?"

"Yes. They come from long ways. Sometimes he goes to them, for he knows when he is needed."

The renown that builds up about a successful aboriginal healer is sometimes remarkable. In traveling around northern New South Wales collecting accounts of aborigines' psychical beliefs and experiences, my wife and I were told many stories about the powers of one particular healer.

A light-caste stockman, so sophisticated that he did not speak the native dialect, told us he was a member of a town football team which was captained by the local police constable.

"I don't believe much in the old-time ways," he told us, "but there's one old fellow who cured me last year. I was getting ready for a game of football, and I went down to the creek before the match and got 'spruced up' a bit. During the match I fell over and hurt my knee, and I couldn't play any more."

(We learned later that the boy had apparently displaced a knee cartilage and the release of the synovial fluid had caused severe swelling.)

"Well, that night the knee hurt a lot, and my people sent for this old fellow they say is clever. He came along and looked at the knee, and he said to me, 'You bin swimmin' in the creek.' I said 'Yes.' I don't know how he could have known that. He said, 'You shouldn't swim in the creek there; it's full of spirits and one of them has caught you.'

"I got real frightened when he told me this in the old-time way, but he said, 'I can cure you.' Then he rubbed my knee and brought out a little bone. He said this was the bad magic."

"Could you see where the bone came out?"

"It came out of my knee but there was no mark because he did it the old-time clever way the old fellows can."

"Did you get better?"

"He told me I could walk and sure enough I could, and it didn't hurt no more. The pain went away right then, and next day all the swelling was gone."

The substance of the boy's account was later confirmed by the police officer and the local doctor.

"What was the name of the old fellow?" we asked.

"Fred Cowlin."

A young man at Woodenbong, Peter Briggs, told us that he had for some time been suffering with a chest complaint which the local white doctor said was pleurisy, and he had been having penicillin injections but had felt little relief.

One morning, just before we interviewed him, he had been suffering great pain and a visiting clever-man was sent for. The old man was his tribal uncle.

"He said to me that I had been swimming in the creek and that I had been caught by some of the clever things that are there," Peter Briggs said. "I was swimming in the creek because it was hot.

"He looked at my chest and rubbed it. Then he put his mouth to it and sucked and took two things out of his mouth. I didn't see them. I think they were bones."

"Did you feel any better then?"

"He told me the pain would go away and I would sleep well—and it's true. I feel lots better now."

"Do you know of any other cures by this man?"

"Yes. He cures lots of peoples, and he can travel quick in the old-time way. He's about the cleverest fellow I know."

We asked Peter Briggs to tell us about one of the doctor's cures that he knew about.

"Well, there was that woman at Pretty Gully called Lillie Dunn. She was living with one of the Walker boys who's a bit clever, too, and he told her not to go walking about by herself. But she didn't take no notice of him and she got awful sick.

"Her people rang up Tabulam Station [about ten miles distant] and asked them to send out that same old fellow that cured me because they thought Lillie Dunn would die. They said he would come out in no time and, sure enough, he did."

"How long did it take him?"

"He was there in a flash."

"An hour?"

"No, less than that."

"Half an hour?"

"No. No time."

"A quarter of an hour?"

"No. No time."

"Five minutes?"

"No, just a minute."

"How did he travel?"

"With his clever things."

"What did he do when he got there?" we asked.

"He told Lillie Dunn she had got a clever thing in her and it was hurting her. He took a stone from her body. It was about the size of a plover's egg. She got better soon after."

"What was the old fellow's name?"

"Fred Cowlin."

Gordon Close was another native we interviewed in the same area. Gordon was a light native, about a quarter-caste we thought, who had adjusted well to the western way of life, owned a motorcar and, on the surface, showed little belief in magic. However, after having several teeth extracted by a dentist at Kyogle, he returned with his face swollen and in great pain. He told us that he had said to his father, Tom

Close, "Send for old Grandad," as he needed relief, and some patent medicines he had taken had proved useless.

"Well, old Grandad came along. He looked at my face but he didn't say anything. He went away and came back with a sheet of newspaper. He put this on the floor. Then he sucked my face. He sucked it for a long time and then he spat on the newspaper. I looked down and there was blood. Three times he spat blood onto the paper. Then he walked away without saying anything."

"And did you feel any better?"

"I felt better straightaway. The pain was gone. I could hear my father talking to old Grandad outside for about half an hour, and when he came back all the swelling was gone."

"And who is 'old Grandad'?"

"Why, Fred Cowlin, of course." Then he went on. "You must have heard about my old grandad. He cures all the people. There was that time that old Bendy Williams from Cooktown in Queensland gave me a pointing bone made by some wild blackfellow up north. You heard about that, didn't you?

"Rory, my brother, got hold of the bone one time and the power in it got him. He went mad. He tried to hatchet some of the people on the station here. All the people locked themselves in their houses while Rory went round, with a mad look in his eye, looking for someone to kill with the ax.

"The manager got the police and they caught him. He was taken to Grafton Jail. They put him in a padded cell. The white people couldn't quieten him down so old Grandad was sent for.

"He went to the jail and saw Rory in the cell. I don't know what he did, but Rory got quiet straightaway. Grandad said he took away the magic that had got in him from the pointing bone. The white people couldn't explain how he did it."

We had indeed heard the account. The station manager had given it to us in almost precisely the same terms.

Such were the stories about the powers of old Fred Cowlin, and there were many of them. His fame as a healer among aboriginal people spread over hundreds of square miles of northern New South Wales and southern Queensland. He is one of the last of the Upper Clarence River doctors still living.

We met old Fred at Tabulam, where he was living with his wife, Bella, in a tiny canvas and bag shelter a quarter of a mile or so from the other natives on the settlement. Sharing the little hut with the old couple were thirty or more dogs, for Fred's totemic animal is the dingo and he is obliged to care for all dogs. The police officer took us to Fred, and as we approached his hut he came out, trembling with fear, and holding in the palm of his outstretched hand a stone with strange markings on it.

"Have you ever seen a stone like this?" said Fred.

I examined it closely. It was an old-fashioned fancy glass paperweight, with an intricate colored pattern cast in the glass. (We learned later that it was one of his clever stones— "a very savage fella," the officer assured us.)

Fred was small and frail. It was many months before he was at ease in our presence, but in visiting him constantly over the years a warm friendship has developed. We could not guess Fred's age, and he certainly did not know it. By reference to elderly white people in the town, who had known him as an elderly man in their youth, we estimated him to be at least ninety and probably one hundred.

His wife, Bella, was even more timid than Fred on first acquaintance, but she was equally avid in her quest for "baccy." Cigarettes offered to her were broken up and rammed into an old pipe. If, during any of our visits to the couple, she happened to get any more cigarettes or tobacco from us than her husband, she hopped about merrily with a wheezy laugh.

We noticed that, although Bella could apparently see quite

well with both eyes, one of them had at some time been damaged. We asked the police officer about it, not imagining that this would produce one of the most interesting little stories about aboriginal ailments and healing that we had, up to that time, encountered.

The policeman took off his white pith helmet and wiped the perspiration from his brow. He was a big man and Fred, we had noticed previously, seemed only to come to a little above his waist.

"Interesting story, that. There was once an old aboriginal doctor lived and practiced in this district. Most powerful fellow, the natives tell me. Name of Fred Ferguson. Well, Bella was married to Ferguson years ago—aboriginal marriage, of course. Ferguson was much older than Bella and inordinately proud of his young and, I suppose, attractive wife. Pretty jealous of her, too, I gather. Told her, amongst other things, that if she married again after his death, she would go blind.

"Ferguson died and it wasn't long after that Bella teamed up with Fred Cowlin, here. Became his wife—and went blind.

"Interesting coincidence, if you like—I don't know much about these things. Fred and Bella were camped at Baryulgil then, where the asbestos mines had just started. She was blind for some years, I gather. Used to wander pitifully over the asbestos diggings. Seems no doubt she really couldn't see.

"Well, one day she fell into a hole at the diggings. The shock must have done something to her, for she completely recovered her sight."

Lyn and I began to discuss parallel clinical cases of neurotic paralysis and subsequent recovery in the white community. But the policeman motioned us to silence.

"Only half the story," he smiled. "Don't know what the value of old Fred Ferguson's curse could have been, but Bella started to go blind again. I saw her at about this time. Something that looked like a cataract was growing over one eye.

"Old Fred here is a doctor amongst his people, as you know. I saw him one day take a twig and flick that growth over her eye clean off. Now, as far as I know, she can see as well as I can."

Fred was not, of course, the only aboriginal doctor about whom accounts were recorded. There were some, including women, both in Central Australia and the coastal areas, about whom interesting and sometimes spectacular stories were told. Fred, however, was himself the source of a great deal of information on the theory and practice of aboriginal healing. Much that he told us confirmed what had been recorded by anthropologists, some was new. He threw light on the methods of all doctors, for their practices are essentially the same throughout Australia. It was he who clearly stated the animistic background against which cures are effected and stated his justification for methods used; he emphasized, in his own way, that although there is a knowledge of physical causes of many ailments the final cure is almost invariably animistic.

For it is in an animistic atmosphere that Australian aborigines live. It is an atmosphere in which superstition can and does thrive, but it is also one of mental vitality.

The aborigines' world is peopled by spirits. Each man has his spirit; so have trees and rocks and animals. Spirit children wait for their fathers to dream of them before they can be born. The spirits of the dead sometimes manifest themselves. Magic impregnates places and things; there are taboos; it is easy to be "caught" by some of the mysterious forces always about, or to be the victim of sorcery.

Thus, for most ailments, the real causes of which are unknown, there is an animistic explanation. This is inevitable in a people where material culture is still (however sympathetically we may view it) Stone Age. It is not to be condemned, this ready recourse to the mysterious, for it is an attempt to come to grips with the problem of cause and effect. And it is not so long ago, after all, that the germ theory of disease came to be accepted by our society.

Against this background of belief in strange forces the aboriginal doctor practices. He practices with a good deal of success—for which we, viewing his methods objectively, can see the psychological reasons—since he is believed to be able to control these strange forces. He has acquired, usually in special ceremonies sustained over a long period, supernatural powers which he may exercise for the good or evil of other persons as he pleases. This he claims; this other natives believe. His prestige in his own society is something for which we can cite no parallel in ours.

Some of the methods used by the doctor in effecting his cures are comparatively straightforward. The removal, by manual extraction or sucking, of things like stones, bones, or twigs from a native patient is of this character. The doctor has, according to aboriginal belief and legend, a clever-eye. This clairvoyant power, said to be acquired during the long process of his training, enables him to see, he claims, inside the victim and locate the magical object, if there be one, that is causing the distress.

There is no doubt in the native's mind that there are physical objects of a magical nature in his body. There is no doubt in him that the doctor removes the objects; that the spot they come out is unmarked because the operation is a magical one.

To the doctor, however, the real methods are, of course, known. "Extracting" objects with his fingers is simple sleight of hand; "sucking" objects out, he secretes them in his mouth beforehand; the blood that he spits out he gets by lacerating his own mouth and gums.

Bluntly I put it to Fred Cowlin that these were the methods he used, emphasizing my charge by "extracting" a twig from the doctor's own arm. Smilingly he agreed, but immediately stressed the psychological point of view. "They bin get better all the same," he said.

To the doctor the methods are not merely trickery; he sees clearly the psychology involved, and the symbolism, he believes, aids him in exercising mental forces he genuinely believes himself to possess.

Moreover, when a doctor himself falls ill he seeks the services of a fellow practitioner, who uses precisely the same artifices in treating him, often with the same spectacular results as are achieved with naïve tribal members. Despite the deceit, despite the complete awareness of the mechanics involved, when a doctor has a quartz crystal or bone "removed" from his body by another doctor, or is assured that his stolen soul has been recovered, he responds in just the same way as other natives.

There seems no doubt that the ordinary native really believes that the removal of objects from his body takes place in fact. Owen Anderson, a light-caste native who owns his own home and land, is steadily employed, and reads and writes English with ease, told me about treatment he had had from Fred Cowlin for what appeared to be a cyst in his arm. Fred went through a typical process of rubbing and sucking, eventually spitting blood onto a sheet of newspaper he had placed nearby. The swelling in Anderson's arm went down almost immediately.

I was able to discuss this with Owen frankly. "Do you think that Fred really sucked blood out of your arm?"

"Yes. Of course. I saw it on the newspaper."

"Was there any mark on your arm where the blood might have come out?"

"No. He did it the clever way."

"Owen," I said, "white people don't believe that it is possible that blood could come out of your arm like that without leaving a mark. Other aborigines have told me about bones and stones coming out the same way. Don't you think that, to get the blood that seemed to come from your arm, Fred may have tricked you by biting his tongue or gums?"

"No. I'm sure the blood came out of my arm. The swelling went down. That proves it, doesn't it?"

So profound is native acceptance of the reality of magical extractions, that their evidence sometimes tends to be colored by their belief and the memory of an experience embellished to conform to the magic pattern.

When the old Birri full blood from Bowen (Queensland), Harry Monsell, told me about seeing a doctor suck a stone about the size of a hen's egg from the body of a woman who was suffering from abdominal pains, I put it to him that the doctor had deceived them.

"Oh, no," he said, firmly. "That same old doctor I saw once fix up a man who had a chest pain. He said the man had got a porcupine [echidna or spiny anteater] spike in him. The doctor sang a song, and I saw with my own eyes the quill come out of the body of the man."

"Do you mean that it seemed to come directly out of his flesh?"

"Yes."

"Did the doctor perhaps pull it out?"

"No. He just sang and it came up. When it came right out, it fell down onto the ground."

"Was there any blood or any mark where the quill had come out?"

"No, there was no mark. The man got better."

There are some variants in treatment that resemble the "psychic" cures found in a number of guises throughout the world. A Gidabul native, Danny Sambo, although not a tribal doctor in the generally accepted sense, claimed to be especially adept at curing headaches. He said he simply stroked the patient's head and "thought" the ache away.

"Anyone can cure like that," declared Sambo.

Danny Sambo also uses a fur cord to effect certain cures.

He attaches one end of the cord to the afflicted part and then applies his lips to the cord. He sucks along the cord from the patient to the free end, which he sometimes places in a container. Into this he may spit blood.

As a lay practitioner Sambo claimed no supernatural assistance, but the conventional doctor is aided in his diagnoses and cures by totemic spirit familiars. Old Fred Cowlin's assistants are dogs; Winjin in Areyonga Valley had lizards. These assistants are like spirits which reside in the doctor and do his bidding. They are usually acquired, like the clever-eye, at the doctor-initiation ceremonies.

The doctor is aided not only by the widespread and profound belief in magic of his patients, but also by their stoical attitude to pain and discomfort. Young men are trained during their initiation to steel themselves against such painful practices as subincision, depilation, tooth evulsion, and cicatrization; probably the training is also in the development of the self-induced trance.

Whether or not aborigines feel pain to the same degree as we do is debatable; that they react to it with remarkable indifference is unquestionable. One investigator, Dr. R. Piddington, suggests that aborigines have a much slighter sensibility to pain than we have because in their culture pain has comparatively little social value. It is obvious, of course, that pain has extremely high social value—it is the reaction to it that differs.

My wife and I interviewed an Aranda native at Hermannsburg who had shortly before been speared in the thigh. The barbed head of the spear had not gone right through; so, after breaking off the haft, he pushed the spear farther through, aiding its exit on the other side by cutting his flesh with a razor blade. He had then walked to the mission for assistance.

We asked him if it were painful. For answer he slapped his thigh and smilingly assured us he felt no discomfort.

As well as being a leech, the aboriginal doctor is often a detective and coroner as well. He is called on to diagnose the cause of deaths, particularly when black magic is suspected. There is a variety of ways in which he may do this, such as running dust through his fingers and claiming to see the face of the murderer in the pattern it makes. Or he may gaze into the smoke of a fire. This is rather like crystal gazing or, on an even more mundane level, teacup reading. Probably a mild form of trance is induced, and the doctor may or may not exercise some sort of clairvoyant ability. The judgment he makes is almost invariably a popular one; a wily clever-man usually nominates a tribally acceptable scapegoat.

Kurnai clever-men sometimes cut off the hand of a corpse and spoke to it asking it to indicate the murderer. Natives claim to have seen such hands twist and point!

Clever-men may speak to the corpse itself (claiming, of course, to be communicating with his spirit) and ask him to name his murderer. Doctors claim, therefore, to act as mediums.

Lyn and I asked Joe Culham, an elderly Mullanjarli native, if he had heard about psychic inquests of this sort among his people.

"Oh, yes," he said. "Many times I have seen the old clever-fellows talking to the bodies as they were being taken to the grave. The body was carried slung on a pole with two men walking in front and two behind. Old clever-fellows would walk beside and talk to the body. The body would answer, too."

"You mean it would speak?"

"No, it would twist. Just like speaking, I suppose. It used to tell them what they wanted to know."

"Did you, yourself, ever see this, Joe?" we asked.

"Oh, yes. Once I was carrying the pole on my shoulder. The clever-fellow was walking along talking away. He was saying, 'Who did this to you? Show us who killed you.' I was right behind the body and I saw it move. I felt the pole twist on my shoulders."

"Perhaps you were walking over rough ground, or one of the others made the body seem to move," we suggested.

Joe denied this vigorously. "Oh, no," he said. "I'm certain the body twisted—I'd seen it other times, too—and I felt that my footsteps were being guided."

"What do you mean?"

"Well, my footsteps seemed to lead me—and the others said the same, later, too. I couldn't help myself. They forced me. We followed the way the body made us go, and we walked straight up to one man and stopped.

"I don't mind telling you I was frightened. The clever-man said, 'You did this. You killed this man!'"

"What did the native say?"

"He looked at the ground and said nothing."

"Do you think he had killed the man?"

"The dead man told us he did," replied Joe Culham, as if this were the final proof.

"And then——?"

"He was killed."

"You said you had seen other occasions when a corpse being carried on a pole twisted after the doctor spoke to it. Did it ever happen that the corpse didn't move?"

"Yes. This happened once or twice."

We asked what happened then.

"Well, the old clever-fellow could look at the dead man's light and tell from that who the killer was."

Joe went on to explain that a clever-man, and sometimes ordinary natives as well, could see a sort of psychic light about a dead man's grave for a short time after his death, usually about three days. The clever-men could speak to this light, and it would guide them to the murderer. Joe had not seen this psychic light but he knew that Clara Williams had.

Clara Williams was a cheerful woman, nearly eighty years of age, and proud of her neat little cottage on the station and the large number of state wards she had taken under her wing. Until her recent death we had had many talks with her about the psychic life of her people, for she had lived with her tribe for a number of years and, despite her age, was active, mentally alert, and a valuable informant.

Clara paused from her housework to greet us.

"We have heard that you once saw a strange light after a person's death. It is supposed to have something to do with the person's *wogai* [spirit]. We want to know if you can tell us about it."

"Yes, it was long times ago, when I was only a little girl. My uncle was caught by a man in the tribe who hated him, and he died."

"When you say he was caught, do you mean that someone made magic against him?"

"That's right. We didn't know who at the time, though. When my uncle died, we all moved camp because the dead man's *mogwee* stays and haunts the place."

"Is the *mogwee* the same as the *wogai?*"

"No. The *mogwee* is a sort of ghost. The *wogai* is a spirit."

Such are the subtle distinctions made by aborigines.

"When we moved camp, we stayed one night by a big log. We lay down to sleep with our feet towards the log and then I saw the light. Everyone saw the light. It came along the log top, and as it came closer I could see my uncle's face in it. It went past where I was and then it stopped. It stopped opposite a man. Then it went out.

"Next morning my aunt went straight up to this man, and she said to him, 'You did this thing! You did the killing! We have been shown that it was you!'

"This man got pretty scared being found out like this, I suppose. He ran away and we never saw him again. That's the only time I ever seen the light. Most times if a killing happens, an old clever-man tells who done it. Them old clever-fellows always knows, you know."

On the narrow green swath that is the foot of Areyonga Valley, with rocky red walls rising steep on either side, is the camp of the Pitjendadjara—a number of tiny, grass *wurlies*. One of them stands slightly apart from the others. It is the home of Winjin, their doctor.

There is no brass plate on the door—there is, indeed, no door. The doctor has no instruments apart from his own body and mind. Yet he performs miracles and his people depend on him. They respect him and they hold him in awe.

As Tjalkalieri and I walked by his *wurlie*, we saw him sitting in the shade with his tiny son on his knees. The child was pulling at his beard and gurgling with delight as the big man pretended to bite him. Winjin gave us a cheery wave.

"He's a pretty clever fellow, that Winjin," said Tjalkalieri, and then, after a moment's thought, asked, "Have you got fellows like that where you come from?"

"No," I said. "We've got no one quite like him."

CHAPTER 6

The Magic Cord

The chanting had been going on all night. Booming bull-roarers (the voice of Baieme, the god) had echoed through the hills, now here, now there, punctuating the tuneless songs. There was a hollow tapping of wood on wood.

Now all was silent; even the night birds had no song. Ghostly mists floated in the valleys, lit by the first light of dawn. In a small clearing, completely naked, lay two boys, fearful, apprehensive. They had heard the songs, but the singers were unseen, they had heard the voice of the great Baieme calling to them, and his voice had seemed to come from the bowels of the earth. They knew that soon would come the great trial to make them men. The silence was tantalizing. This was their initiation, the "making."

For as many moons as their hands had fingers the two of them had been preparing for this supreme moment. For the first few months older relatives, specially appointed, had been instructing them in tribal lore and ritual, in the meaning of manhood, on their responsibilities and their rights as men. They had been shown some of the sacred tribal churinga. Then some of the doctors had taught them about themselves, shown them how injuries can be borne without pain, taught them something of the control of fear—but they were afraid now. The doctors had introduced them to an inner life of contemplation that, to the aborigines, is a mark of manhood.

There followed for them a long period of isolation from the tribe with but short intervals of contact with a few men of the totem when cicatrices had been cut and weals burned on their chest, back, and arms. They had lived amidst comparative plenty in the bush but were allowed to hunt and eat only a few of the animals about them, and subsist on a restricted variety of roots and berries. Despite hunger they dared not violate the taboos for they knew that this privation was necessary to become a man. And they knew, too, that back in the main camp the doctors knew what they were doing, could see them with their clever-eyes, or were perhaps floating unseen above them on their magic cords watching them, always watching them.

They were being watched now.

Suddenly, from behind them, out of the silence, came the booming "oowah, oowah" of a bull-roarer and, as if in answer, "oowahwah" from another directly ahead. Then, all round them, booming, filling their ears with vibrating, restless tempo, came the roar. And into the pale light stepped a man, his body covered with clay and ocher, feathers and blood, whirling a sacred bull-roarer on its cord of human hair, dancing slowly, deliberately, toward them. His body quivered and the white cockatoo down seemed like a restless cloud clinging to him.

Other men came from the shadows, all painted, some twirling roarers, some with spears. There were dancers, too, their bodies gleaming yellow as the dawn light warmed.

Abruptly the noise ceased and before them, as if coming from nowhere, stood a huge man at whom all the other men looked with awe. Or was it a man? Was it Baieme come from the Eternal Dream Time?

He looked closely at them and they could see fires burning in his eyes. "Watch me," he said. He lay on his back. His body gave a shiver and his mouth opened. Some of the men gasped almost inaudibly. From his mouth the boys saw a thing come forth, a live thing that was not a snake, nor was it a cord. But it looked like a cord and moved like a snake. Slowly it issued from the gaping, quivering jaws, the length of a man's finger but not so thick. It moved about on the man's face and became longer, almost as long as a man's arm. It left his mouth and crawled in the grass. Then it returned to the man's body.

After a time the big man left and there was another man before them, an old man whose gums were toothless and whose beard was very white, like the cockatoo down. This man was telling them to look at him, showing them a large, bright crystal that stole the light from the dawn and dazzled their eyes. The old man was speaking to them but the words were only sounds whose meaning was lost in the warmth of the sun he held in his hand. Soon the boys felt something moving on their bodies, things that felt like snakes and spiders. One of the boys breathed deeply and relaxed, sinking into a state of repose that was almost sleep. He felt these things, but he was not afraid.

The other lad had begun to tremble. Perspiration broke out on his cold skin and he became tense. There seemed to be a multitude of reptiles about him, sliding over his body. He thought he felt the sharp stab of fangs in his leg and it went numb. For a moment a cry choked itself in his throat; then he jumped to his feet and screamed, shivered, and screamed again. Some men grasped him and led him sobbing away. He had failed. He would not be "made." Death must now follow his disgrace. Grim-faced men returned silently to the clearing and the drama went on.

The remaining lad then witnessed a series of displays. Clever-men appeared to lie on their backs and clever-ropes exuded from their mouths, their navels. The cords seemed to rise into the air, and the old fellows climbed hand over hand up them to treetop height. Then some of them moved from the top of one tree to the top of another by means of the cords, which swayed out into space. The boy had been told that clever-men could travel vast distances in no time with the aid of such cords; now he was seeing for himself some of these marvelous things.

Some of the doctors walked straight to the trunks of big eucalyptus trees and appeared to melt into them, reappearing a moment later on the other side.

The boy saw the doctors produce from within themselves great numbers of gleaming quartz crystals, grinning as the wet crystals that seemed to come from within them were taken from between pituri-stained teeth. Each old doctor formed a small pile of crystals beside him. These, too, were part of his power, symbols of the sacred water that each had acquired during his making as a clever-man. With these the doctor could perform many miracles: the crystals warned him of the approach of enemies, he was assisted by them in making his cures, he could project one or more into an enemy and thus kill him. There seemed to be a friendly competition between the old doctors to see who could produce the greatest number of crystals.

The boy was conscious that old scars on his back and chest were being opened and fresh cicatrices were being cut. The oldest of the doctors, those who had the greatest number of crystals, those who had climbed the trees with their cords, or passed through them, clustered about him and his "making" was completed.

For a moment he saw before him again the old man with the brilliant crystal in his hands.

Then the atmosphere changed. Men formed into little, chattering groups and his tribal relatives crowded round the boy. There was laughing and joking and, when some of the secret tribal markings had been removed, the men made their way slowly back to the main camp.

This is how initiation ceremonies were described for me by Tjalkalieri and other natives. Naturally the pattern differed from area to area and from tribe to tribe, but basically it was the same. A native who has been "through the ring" (initiation ceremonies on the coast occur at circular *borah* grounds) or "given the rule" is highly thought of in detribalized groups of aborigines now. There were many interesting features about these descriptions, and one that certainly required investigation was that of the magic cord.

Such magic cords or magic ropes figure prominently in aboriginal mythology and are related to the mythological snakes, especially the rainbow snake, that occur in the vast explanatory legends of aboriginal lore.

In these accounts of initiations I had collected were the descriptions modified to conform with legend, or did those who took part really believe that they had seen cords exuded by clever-men and a variety of feats performed with them? I was not able to obtain a clear-cut, unequivocal answer to this problem from the tribal desert natives.

But the coastal natives threw a great deal of light on the matter. We vigorously pursued an investigation of the magic cord among these people. Most of the information came through a comprehensive questionnaire by which the natives were asked about a wide variety of magical experiences and beliefs.

Half the natives interviewed had actually seen a magic cord, they claimed.

Robin Walker, last of the Upper Clarence River natives to be initiated, we found in silent contemplation beneath a huge gum tree.

At his initiation, Robin said, he had seen a doctor climb to the height of such a tree by climbing hand over hand up a magic cord that he had made come from his mouth.

"It was a wonderful thing," he said, "and such we do not see now. The power has gone. It is true that these old fellows can still do clever things, but when I was a boy they were very great, very clever."

"We heard that you were clever, Robin."

"No," he denied. "But my brother Eric or that old fellow Edward Derry, called Mumbi, might tell you more. They say Mumbi has a clever cord."

We did not see his brother Eric, but we heard about him from a native living a hundred miles to the north, Owen Anderson. Owen, a well-educated native, had seen Eric Walker produce a magic cord only a few years previously.

"We were walking along in the bush—three or four of us—talking about the old-time powers of the doctors. Eric Walker said to us, 'I got a clever rope. I'll show it to you.' He lay down on the ground and his face was all twisted up and he breathed heavy. We all watched him and I was pretty frightened.

"Soon we saw something coming out of Eric's mouth. It was alive and moving about."

"How thick was it?"

"It was no thicker than your little finger and sandy in color. It had a sort of blunt head. It moved about like a snake. We were all awful frightened; then it went back and Eric woke up again."

"How long was it?"

"We only saw about six inches that time but a couple of days later, when we were all together again, Eric said, 'You fellows ought to see all that clever-rope of mine' and he lay down again.

"Well, the whole rope came out this time. It was as long as your arm and it crawled about in the grass like it was alive. Then it went back into his body."

"You're sure it wasn't a snake—you'd recognize a snake?"

"Oh, nothing like a snake, no."

"Or an earthworm?"

Owen laughed aloud.

"If you had seen it, you would know it wasn't a worm. It wasn't the color of a worm."

"You know what we mean by hypnotism, Owen? You've told me that you've seen white men at theaters making others go to sleep and seem to see things that are not there. Would Eric Walker have done this, do you think?"

"Oh, no." Owen laughed again. "No, not that. This was real clever stuff."

"I see. Did Eric tell you beforehand what you were going to see, and then you saw it?"

"Yes."

Here was a suggestion of hypnotism at work.

Mumbi (which means simply "cousin") we found at Tabulam. He was old and frail, and reluctant to talk about magic of any sort; certainly there was little he would say about the magic cord. Yes, he had seen one. The doctor who had it used it to stop rain. It was about a foot long and black. The doctor had to pull it out of his mouth, but when he did, the rope crawled around in the grass of its own accord.

"We heard that you have such a cord, Mumbi."

"No."

"We heard that you were pretty clever and you had a cord that helped you."

"I am not clever. I am old and the cleverness has gone."

Natives at Woodenbong, however, were not so reluctant to discuss the mysterious cord. My wife and I had now been talking about their magic with them at intervals over more than four years.

One afternoon we were conducting some of our tests on a cottage veranda and paused briefly from these to talk about the cord. There was quite a crowd on the veranda—Danny Sambo, a full-blood initiate of the Gidabul tribe, Bert Mercy, a Nogwadjil from the region of Coff's Harbor, Joe Culham, a seventy-one-year-old Mullunjarli native, and a number of young men, mostly of the Bundulung-speaking group.

Bert Mercy said he had often seen magic cords. Usually they were black, at other times sandy, and they were never thicker than a single strand of horsehair.

"That's true," said Danny Sambo. "Just like black threads."

"Tom Kenny!" he called, and a native passing by walked over to us. "Tom, you seen them doctors' threads they can bring out. Tell us about them."

"Yes, I seen them cords all right. I seen doctors with them crawling all over their faces, just like live, black cobwebs."

"You seen them no thicker than that? I seen them like a piece of fence wire. I touched them, too—all slimy-like they was."

"They say old Fred Cowlin's got one of them," said a youth.

"That's true," exclaimed another youth, Owen Morgan. "They say he was riding it one day in the sky and he caught up with a jet plane."

A smile must have passed my lips.

"It's true, mister," he expostulated. "That old fellow's as clever as can be."

"You believe he could catch up with a jet plane, Owen?" I asked.

Murmurs from the group assured me there was no doubting Owen's belief (though he was a young, sophisticated caste native) or their own.

"Bert was telling us about those he had seen," I said, and Bert Mercy went on.

"The doctors find their cords in creeks," he said. "I have seen them myself in clear waters. But you only find them when you're not looking for them. When the doctors find them, they tie a knot in them and take them into themselves. Then they get cleverer."

"How would that make them cleverer?"

"They can cure people who are sick, make storms, travel long ways in the skies——"

"And keep danger away," interrupted Joe Culham.

"And catch people," said Tom Kenny.

All eyes turned toward him. "Yes. I seen people caught with a cord. My grandfather had a cord. It was about four feet long, and he told me he used it to catch people, and when he did this they died."

"Did you ever see the cord, Tom?"

"Yes, lots of times. I seen my grandfather break up a storm with that same cord. He took it out and whirled it round his head."

"Did it seem to be alive?"

"Yes. And it had a flat head like some of those snakes."

So the accounts were recorded. And from these eyewitness accounts we built up a picture of the cord that differed somewhat from the second-hand or mythologically embellished accounts.

Mostly the cord was inches long rather than feet, and a couple of feet at most, sandy to black in color, very thin rather than thick, and seemed to be alive. Usually it came from the doctor's mouth, and sometimes he pulled it from his mouth and sucked it back again later.

Further enlightening information came from Willie Mackenzie, a Yinliburra native, who said he had seen a cleverman take a thin cord, about nine inches long, from his mouth. It was like a fine thread. He held it over the glowing coals of a fire, and it crawled up into his hand. Then he returned it to his mouth. The cord seemed to tie itself into knots, he said.

With basic data like this we were left with a number of things to explain. For example, could all or part of the reports be explained by hypnotism? Did the informants really see something? If they did, could the ordinary sleight-of-hand tricks of doctors explain what they saw?

Could the cords be, for example, sinews of animals, or perhaps living creatures?

This is the answer we tentatively advanced. It was not

complete since it did not explain all the aspects of the magic cord, but it did explain a good many of them and might certainly have been the genesis of the more startling accounts that may have followed exaggeration and modification to conform to a customary pattern.

In bodies of fresh water throughout Australia a fine, threadlike worm, *Gordius,* may be found. (Bert Mercy said the cord came from sacred waters.) It is unusual in that it grows within a host (a beetle or grasshopper) and emerges as a fully grown adult. So that one day a pool may be completely clear and the next have numbers of writhing, threadlike worms in it.

It would seem that doctors, at an appropriate time, might swallow and later regurgitate these, or at least secrete them in the mouth. (Bert had also said the doctors take them in, and before doing so, tie a knot in them; perhaps that had some significance.) At the appropriate moment in a demonstration the worms crawl forth from the doctor's mouth or are pulled out (as Mumbi and others had said) and are later sucked back in (as Tom Kenny said).

This explanation was plausible. If a demonstration of a magic cord could be obtained by a white man, and the cord found to be a *Gordius* worm, then the evidence would be very much stronger.

But the existing evidence was complicated in a rather strange way. The phenomenon of the magic cord as recounted by aborigines closely resembled the phenomenon of ectoplasm reported by spiritualists and others and the stories throughout mythology (to which the *Gordius,* which is found in other parts of the world, has no doubt made its contribution), so that the mundane explanation advanced might not be the complete one.

In the case of the aborigines it appeared not to be "all done with mirrors." But was it all done with hypnotism? Or was there yet another possible answer?

We pushed ahead with our investigation but seemed to make no significant advance.

Then one midsummer day I visited Woodenbong for a few hours to check on the details of a few stories I had collected earlier in the year. I had driven the hundred miles to the settlement from Brisbane. It was hot, the country dry and dusty, the air alive with the noise of thousands of cicadas. I found the manager away and the station almost deserted. My most valued informants were away visiting friends. I passed the time of day with a few natives and prepared to drive back to Brisbane.

Then Tom Kenny came up to the car.

"You know that thing you was wanting to see?" he said. "The cord?"

"Yes. There's a fellow name of Alex Freeburn here that knows a fellow staying in the town now; come walkabout from the south. He says he'll show you the cord."

I took the other man into the township, and we sought out the man reputed to have the cord. He was called "Brandy" and I could smell why.

The three of us sat in the shade of a huge gum a short distance away from a small native hut. After a few minutes of inconsequential chatter, "Brandy" looked into Alex' eyes and said, "I'll show you the cord."

I sat quietly and watched. Keeping his eyes closely fastened on the other native, "Brandy" lifted his fingers to his open mouth, put them inside, and then brought them out again as though pulling something, something I could not see. He was breathing heavily and perspiration was running down his face. Alex was watching, apparently absorbed—and apparently seeing something.

"Brandy" brought his fingers out about a foot from his lips, and then moved them slowly back again.

He spoke, and his words were very significant.

"Did you see the cord?"

"Yes, I seen it," said Alex enthusiastically and, I thought, honestly.

But there was no cord. I saw not a thing.

When I told "Brandy," he at first appeared disappointed, but then he said with determination, "You'll see it this time, all right."

In a few moments he went through a similar procedure but this time his fingers stayed in his mouth a little longer. Then he slowly and carefully brought them forth, drawing out a thin thread of saliva. He managed to draw this out to a length of about five inches. It was cleverly done, but as a demonstration of a magic cord it was most disappointing.

Alex was unquestionably hypnotized. He was probably able genuinely to report that he had seen something, and this something he had seen, which he had been told he would see, was his own conception of a magic cord.

The question of the magic cord is not yet fully resolved. I am thoroughly convinced that hypnotism plays a major part and is probably associated with the *Gordius* worm, or animal sinews, or spittle manipulation, or some other such form of deception.

CHAPTER 7

How Magicians Are Made

The urge to "go walkabout" is one of the most interesting (and sometimes exasperating) traits of the aborigines. If a field worker is prepared to move around the Australian wilds with a group of natives, he can be sure of gathering worth-while material; for when this impulse to travel grips a native and he is on the move, he seems to be in a more communicative mood than usual.

This was certainly the case with Tjalkalieri, and when he suggested a visit to his tribal home near Ayers Rock, two hundred miles to the west of Areyonga Valley, we were tempted to accept. He even drew crude maps consisting of circles and whorls, duplicating those found on the sacred *churinga*, by which he said he would guide us. (The maps showed, in a stylized form, the natural features and sacred areas of the country we would have crossed. To the uninformed they would have appeared as intricate, interesting, and artistic designs.)

But, as no really first-class camel team, such as would have been needed for the trip, was available, we compromised with a much shorter excursion to Palm Valley, which we could manage easily in a couple of days, and by horse.

We took three horses. Tjalkalieri rode the little black mare, Lyn a plodding, docile beast that carried her and our

114

camp gear. I shared my saddle alternately with Kinchika and Tjalkalieri's "half-caste kid," Nugget. More often the boys walked, excitedly exploring the fertile valley together.

Tjalkalieri was happy. We took two rifles with us—a .303 and a .22—for there were "plenty kangaroo 'n euro" in the valley.

The approach to Palm Valley was through wild, red, rocky gorges whose floors and slopes were sprinkled with saltbush and spinifex. It was barren country, scarred with misshapen boulders and massive, primeval rocky outcrops.

But the valley itself was fertile, unbelievably rich in exotic vegetation. Strange palms that grow nowhere else in the world, and which have defied transplanting, flourished here. Clear, fresh water gurgled the valley's entire length through reedy rock pools covered with wild ducks. There were massive amphitheaters, on whose bare rock walls kangaroos and euros abounded; deep gullies where carpet snakes and giant perentie lurked; pools that sparkled with tiny, silvery fish.

If desert natives had a heaven on earth, this was it. Indeed, their interpretation of paradise is a "place where clear waters flow and the sun shines all day."

It was not surprising that Palm Valley played a big part in native lives and was associated with much of their folklore and magic. Here, as in Areyonga Valley (which is really the other end of Palm Valley) were rock pools in which the fabulous rainbow snakes, sources of much of the aboriginal doctors' powers were said to live.

Rainbow snakes are but one source of the aboriginal doctors' powers. These also come from sacred waters and the sacred waters are symbolized by quartz crystals which, in theory, doctors take into themselves at their making and produce on subsequent occasions to kill, cure, or hypnotize.

Just as in our own society where there are usually basic requirements for admission to the various professions, religious offices, and so on, so aboriginal society has adopted procedures for apprenticeship, training, and admission to its higher degrees. Although we would probably prefer to believe that our requirements are based on sound, practical grounds, they do, in fact, derive their status largely from tradition; the aborigines' requirements are sanctioned by their mythology.

As Tjalkalieri and I sat on the sandy bank of a stream in Palm Valley waiting for a euro we had shot earlier in the day to cook, I asked him how doctors acquired their strange powers. He began by explaining in terms of mythology. The doctor is selected by the great spirits, who bid him leave the tribe and come to sacred waters as his spiritual ancestors had done. Here they ritually kill him, often with pointing bones or magic spears, take out his insides and give him a new set. They sing his magic cord and crystals into him, and when he recovers he realizes he has new powers and returns to camp. He must not use his powers, however, until at least a year has passed.

The significance of singing, which accompanies nearly all types of magic, might well be mentioned here. Chants and invocations are familiar to us, mostly in a religious setting; some fragments of magical chants and spells have persisted as frank superstitions; for example, the recitation of a verse after a misadventure of some sort. In some places this sort of thing has the genteel description of "folklore." To the aborigines singing is a clear-cut and definite means by which magical powers can be inserted into objects or men, by which supernatural forces can be invoked into action and, sometimes, by which black magic can be removed or nullified.

Tjalkalieri's account of a doctor's making was typical of his descriptions of other ceremonies which mark a change of role. They all reflected the generalized pattern of transition rites (as they occur in anthropological accounts) where the central experience is death or at least a profound state of trance.

Tjalkalieri appeared to deliberate for some time. He stirred the sand round the euro with a stick, drew a few aimless whorls in the sand, and came to sit beside me again.

"I remembers," he said. "An old fellow told me one time how he came to be a doctor fellow.

"He told me the story when I was a young man soon after I was made. He said to me: 'When I was a boy, a doctor said to me that I would be clever like him. He took me away from my people into the desert to a spring where only the doctors go. He took some waters from the spring and held them in his hands. As I looked at his hands, the waters became crystals, and he pushed the crystals into my chest.

"'The stones went right into my chest without leaving a mark because he did it the clever way. I felt warm and strong inside me. These stones were to make me clever and to see things that other people cannot see, like the great spirits and peoples who are just dead and are not people but spirits.

"'Later on the doctor fellow and some other old fellows took me away and showed me things. One old fellow brought a cord from out of himself. He tied it to the end of a stick and gave me the stick. He said that it would take me to the Dream Time. He showed me a big crystal and I felt my own crystals rise in me and I was able to take them out of me and they made me feel stronger.

"'The cord on the stick pulled me along. It went into a big boulder and I went after it and came out the other side, and all the men cried out aloud in praise.

"'Then the old men showed me how to ride on the cord, and we went to the clouds and saw great spirits and learned more magic.'

"This was the story the man told me."

Such are the types of fantastic accounts given by medicine men about how they acquire their powers. It would seem they create the fantasy and themselves believe it. In this case the man was selected and prepared by a doctor for his profession. This, indeed, is the most usual way.

In many areas quartz crystals play an important part in the doctor-making ceremonies and subsequently in the activities of the doctor. During the postulant's trance it is supposed often that his head and abdomen are opened, either by attendant clever-men or officiating spirits, and one or more pieces of quartz inserted. This quartz has peculiar psychical qualities, according to aboriginal claims, the principal being that it gives its owner what might be termed X-ray vision, so that he can see into the minds of others and know what they are thinking, probe the bodies of stricken natives for the source of evil magic afflicting them, and see events that are happening at a distance. It is a source of power upon which the clever-man may draw at will. Sometimes, produced by sleight of hand, it can be used as a display of power, or to frighten natives.

What is the peculiar significance of quartz and other unusual stones, such as the small black obsidian bombs called "blackfellows' buttons" found on the Nullarbor Plains? Apart from their pleasing symmetry and comparative rarity, which would make them attractive to natives, I believe they are used extensively for hypnotism.

With few exceptions, the training of a prospective aboriginal doctor begins when he is ten or twelve and culminates in the final transition rites when he is approaching thirty. Even after his making, it may be some years before a native doctor flourishes into the full practice of magical arts. A striking exception to this generalization occurs in a few tribes where lay individuals may, in only about six months, be trained for and actually practice, many advanced forms of magic.

Although training is begun early in his life, the postulant must be a full initiate of the tribe before any of the secrets of magic are imparted to him. This is not in the nature of "matriculation" since all males must undergo the long and exacting period of mental and spiritual training, with attendant physical ordeals, preceding admission to adulthood. The youth who shows himself to be especially adept during the common period of training is more likely to be selected than others who barely fulfill tribal requirements. There is good reason to believe that lads so selected are singled out because they are good hypnotic subjects.

Youths are carefully watched by tribal elders and clevermen in their normal activities, even at play, for indications of an aptitude toward magical office. Boys who tend to dominate their fellows, who show unusually vital personality traits, may be selected for eventual graduation to offices of magic. They may be tested in various ways, sometimes with their knowledge, sometimes surreptitiously. They may, for example, be given special sentences for interpretation, and other "aptitude tests" are administered.

For the lad who wins the approval of the doctors, tentative though the approval may be at this stage, there begins a long period of instruction that might well be described as a spiritual apprenticeship.

Such an apprenticeship Tjalkalieri described as a time when "the boy is taught many things." Danny Sambo, of Woodenbong, however, had exemplified it admirably with a story of a lad who was a veritable "sorcerer's apprentice."

"I seen a boy working for a doctor," said Danny, "and, so help me, it was the cleverest thing I ever seen. It was when an old woman I knew was sick, and they sent for the doctor fellow—old Jimmie McQuiltie it was. He came along and with him was a boy who was about fourteen. Old Jimmie looked at the woman but he didn't say anything.

"Then he looked at the boy and whispered something to him. The boy looked at the woman, and after a while he pointed to her head. Old Jimmie McQuiltie then put the palm of his hand against the woman's forehead and pressed it. He put his mouth there then and sucked, and soon he spat out blood with little stones in it. The woman got better soon after."

"And what about the boy?"

"Why, he was being got ready to be a doctor hisself," said Danny. "In our lingo he was called a *woguragul;* that means a doctor-learner."

As well as spiritual training postulants undoubtedly undergo more mundane instruction in sleight of hand. They would be taught how to secrete bones, stones, and other articles about their person, how to lacerate their gums with crystals and spit out blood, how to look always preternaturally grave, how to practice the gentle art of dissimulation.

At many of the transition rites prospective doctors acquire totemic assistants (much the same as medieval witches' spirit familiars, which were usually toads or cats) who assist them in their magic. They are said, for example, to be able to go on psychic journeys and acquire information for their doctor.

Usually, it would seem, the doctor is in a self-induced trance state. "They go walkabout long ways while doctor sleeps," Tjalkalieri explained.

"One doctor Winjin told me about got his totem this way: his father gave it to him. His father was lizard totem and he made the boy lie on his back. Then the boy knew his father would make him. The father took a lizard out of himself and put it on the boy's chest, and sang a song that made the lizard go right into the boy."

"So the father gave away the lizard he had?"

"The father kept the lizard he had but gave it to his son."

A psychic multiplication presumably was thus supposed to occur.

Natives often claim that they have seen doctors produce these totemic familiars; the animals—lizard, snake, wombat, or what you will—seem to appear from nowhere, but seem real. The doctor may talk to them and they disappear or move off into the bush.

There is, however, at least one account on record in which a white person has presumably seen such a familiar. In her book, *The Euahlayi Tribe*, Mrs. K. L. Parker writes: "A *wirreenun* [clever-man] has the power to conjure up a vision of his particular *yunbeai* [familiar], which he can make visible to those whom he chooses shall see it.

"One day I went to the camp, saw the old man in his usual airy costume, only assumed as I came in sight, a tailless shirt. One of the gins said something to him; he growled an answer; she seemed persuading him to do something. Presently he moved away to a quiet clear spot on the other side of the fire; he muttered something in a sing-song voice, and suddenly I saw him beating his head as if in accompaniment to his song, and then—where it came from I can't say—there beside him was a lizard. That fragment of a shirt was too transparent to have hidden that lizard; he could not have had it up his sleeve, because his sleeves were in shreds. It may have been a pet lizard that he charmed in from the bush by his song, but I did not see it arrive.

"They told me this old man had two *yunbeai*, the other was a snake. He often had them in evidence at his camp, and when he died they were seen beside him; there they remained until he was put into his coffin; then they disappeared and were never seen again. This man was the greatest of our local wizards, and I think really the last of the very clever ones."

One of the most impressive sights I have ever seen was old Fred Cowlin at Tabulam in New South Wales with his totem dogs—real ones. Fred's totem was the dog (actually the dingo) and he had over thirty of the thin, wretched beasts sharing his camp with him and his wife. Fred's dogs were real enough, but he claimed to have two "very big fellows," spirit dogs, who would go on trips for him.

I had been trying to persuade Fred to apply for the old-age pension. For him it was a momentous decision. He called his pack around him and spoke to them at length in his own dialect. They stopped barking and howling and sat round him like a group of well-trained choir boys while he addressed them. When he had finished, their howling broke out anew.

He walked over to me with a smile. "They bin say it hokay," he said.

Fred was never very explicit about how he himself became a doctor. He had hinted that it was because of a strange urge he had experienced. Aranda informants, too, had stressed the significance of an impulse being the starting point of a magical career. I determined to talk to Tjalkalieri on the subject.

"There are men, the Aranda tell me," I said to him, "who are not made doctors by other doctors. They get a feeling they must become doctors."

This rather dramatic method, one involving a specific psychic experience by which a person believes, or at least claims, that he has been called to the profession, does not appear to be common. The event, which may be the seeing and conversing with spirits of the dead, or cult heroes, in dream or trance, may occur spontaneously or may be deliberately sought. If a native has been seeking the experience, he would probably be sleeping near the grave of a former doctor, supposedly a place of great magical potency, or making fires with kangaroo fat to attract the great spirits.

I was thinking of a specific account recorded by H. Basedow in *The Australian Aboriginal* about this very area. The leading clever-man of the western group of the Aranda, Kai-Kai, told Basedow how, when out hunting as a young man, he became detached from the hunting party when tracking a kangaroo he had wounded. Towards sunset he abandoned the pursuit and made for a rock hole in the James Range. On arriving there he threw down his spears and *woomera* and eagerly went to ease his thirst with the cool water. But with his first sip a tadpole entered his mouth. It passed down his throat before he could spit it out and entered his stomach with a painful bump. Each time he tried to drink a tadpole slipped into his mouth and slid into his stomach. Desperate with thirst, he made a last attempt to sip some water—but horror overcame him when he looked into the pool and saw, not his own reflection, but the image of another man. When he looked again he saw that the image was transparent and inside it were a number of rounded pebbles— the same number of pebbles as the tadpoles he had swallowed.

Kai-Kai said he collapsed and slept like a dead man. On waking up he found himself lying among the reeds of a part of the Finke River called Running Waters, and he now quenched his thirst. When he recollected his experience at the rock hole he suddenly realized that the image he had seen was that of a spirit, and he could still feel the pebbles inside him. He realized, too, that he had been ordained a clever-man, and returned to his relatives at the camp.

Tjalkalieri pondered over the story for some time. He pushed his battered hat to the back of his head and ran his fingers through his tousled black curls. It was plain he was thinking deeply, and I thought he was reluctant to answer.

Then he said, "Those doctors proper gammon fellows." By this pronouncement he meant, of course, that he did not consider them to be really doctors, that they who entered the profession this way were charlatans.

However, although the psychic experience is the means by which impostors enter the profession (natives claim that frauds are quickly detected and deposed, or perhaps killed), it is also a legitimate channel.

Anthropologists have likened the secret life of the aborigines, principal aspects of which are associated with doctor making, to our Masonic rituals. Natives zealously guard the secrets, and the real nature of doctor initiation is obscured by ritual and mysticism.

Whatever may happen at these ceremonies, clever-men emerge into aboriginal society as men of outstanding personality, well versed in trickery, sleight of hand, and sly opportunism, first-class hypnotists, politicians, mystics, and intermediaries with the great forces of nature.

III

The Way Love Finds

Yungitcha was a handsome young Pitjen-dadjara initiate. He was slender and graceful. His dark brown hair was carefully oiled with animal fats and tiny ringlets that fell on his neck were held in shape with mud. He preened himself carefully. So striking was the contrast with some other natives in Areyonga Valley that I commented on it one day to Tjalkalieri, when we had returned from Palm Valley.

I was told that Yungitcha was a very eligible bachelor and was "on lookout for girl." I was not particularly interested in the intratribal relationships necessary for marriage so dear to the anthropologist, but I was interested in some of the means that Yungitcha and other young bloods might use in acquiring their mates.

I knew flirting and courtship to be a field in which magical practices of various sorts flourish. Magic operates in realms of uncertainty, and what could be more subject to the vagaries of chance, the influence of potions, charms, and spells, than love?

Did Yungitcha practice any sort of love-magic ritual?

Yes, he did. And with a little explanation from Tjalkalieri, and encouragement from us, he showed Lyn and me a form of ritual. In this he used a love-magic bull-roarer, a small piece of mulga wood, about six inches long, an inch wide, pointed at each end. On one side he had carved his own totemic symbols and on the other those of the girl he wanted.

Adolph (the native with the "cattles") strolled over to join the group. He explained that some educated natives he had known used such a love-magic bull-roarer. They had carved their initials on one side and the girl's on the other. In each case the object had a length of human hair cord passed through a hole in one end.

The purpose of this particular love-magic article and the ritual associated with it was twofold. First, it was intended to awaken interest and desire in the girl of Yungitcha's choice; second, it was to influence the girl's parents to make her available to him.

Close questioning revealed that the charm was believed to be effective no matter how far distant from him the girl might be; something akin to telepathic communication was believed to be established.

"Yes, it's just like ringing a girl up," said Adolph. He had often been to Alice Springs, knew something of telephones and radio, and applied the analogy.

"But does it work, Adolph?"

He assured us that it did. He knew of several cases where a man had twirled such a love-magic bull-roarer and his girl, apparently "hearing" the call, had traveled many miles to her swain.

Indeed, Ronald and Catherine Berndt had given us as an instance a case they had come across in which an aboriginal girl in Arnhem Land had traveled over fifty miles through swampy country after the love call had been sounded.

Spencer and Gillen, early anthropological investigators in Central Australia, were among the first to record such interesting results. "Not long ago at Alice Springs a man called some of his friends together and performed the ceremony and in a very short time the desired woman, who was on this occasion a widow, came in from Glen Helen, about fifty miles to the west of Alice Springs, and the two are now man and wife."

Yungitcha was now anxious to show us something of his ritual. He tucked a wad of pituri behind his ear and crouched down holding the bull-roarer in both hands and uttered a low, monotonous chant.

"Love song," explained Adolph.

Then Yungitcha pointed the stick in one direction, presumably the direction in which he knew the girl was, and finally stood up and whirled it vigorously so that it spun in gleaming arcs at the end of the cord with a low, moaning sound.

"Love call," said Adolph. "Now he ring up. Soon that girl come." There were nods of agreement from the men—all except a sullen young fellow called Selly, on the fringe of the group.

We did not find out if Yungitcha's efforts were successful, but there was no doubting his belief, and that of his companions, in the efficacy of the method.

In some cases where such magical procedures are apparently successful, telepathy could be, and possibly is, responsible. Coincidence and the sly co-operation of friends, on the other hand, are equally acceptable explanations.

In our society sex is rarely approached directly. A whole complex system of social niceties, vagueness and subtlety, and what is virtually a mythology of "romance," precede and obscure the approach to a biological relationship. This is probably a good thing. A similar, but less complex, social restraint is provided for the aborigines by their love magic.

Sex is, of course, important to aborigines. They appear to be aware of the function of sex in reproduction, but this aspect tends to be ignored in their behavior. The spiritual origin of children is of far more importance to aborigines than their parental origin; it is a greater consideration that a woman's husband should dream that she has conceived than that he be responsible for her condition.

Much of love magic is imitative. That is, it pictures a desired event, either in a mime or a drawing. Ocher paintings discovered by the Berndts in Arnhem Land depict pregnant women, couples in sexual activity, individuals with greatly enlarged organs, and so on.

The view might be held, in the absence of better information, that these are merely aimless erotic drawings with no evidence of both desire and intention associated with them. But there is some corroboration of their significance in the fairly widespread practice of, for example, drawing a representation of a woman in the dust and simulating the act of copulation with it, with the native believing that his miming will bring about that situation.

This very belief in the efficacy of a ritual is magical in nature; but usually natives are not content with such passive practices and make specific and direct advances as well.

The advances often follow ritual patterns and many are initiated by women as well as by men. Often they have an element of magic too. Present giving is such a procedure. A plug of tobacco, for example, is used by a woman in an erotic ritual during which it is charmed by being sung and is used in an imitative love-magic act. She or a friend will take the tobacco and drop it before the man's bark shelter or shanty, or openly give it to him.

It is supposed that when he smokes the tobacco he will become dizzy and, even though it may be against his reason or contrary to his normal wishes, seek out the woman and meet her desire.

Although its immediate and usual object is primarily sexual, love magic is a means of obtaining a wife. Other more customary means are by arrangement or by capture. In many tribes magic is a normal and legal method, provided it is practiced between the appropriate groups.

When a native follows a magical procedure sanctioned by tribal custom, the magical element reinforces the effectiveness of this type of advance and tends to sanction any more direct action he may decide on.

If a native wishes a woman to elope with him and follows the appropriate procedures, he is then entitled to enlist the physical support and aid of his relatives in the project. Thus the group co-operates to bring about the wishes of one of its members.

While love magic is practiced along traditional lines and to reinforce the advances made in the case of regular alliances (that is, those that are sanctioned by tribal law), it is also sometimes used by a native to win a mate to whom he is not truly entitled.

This is probably one of the most common causes of disputes among the aborigines, and not merely are individuals involved, but also groups. This often results in a long feud. The woman will go to the group which is ultimately victorious.

My wife and I obtained very little first-hand information in Central Australia on the women's love magic *corroborees.* Men have such *corroborees,* but the women's appear to be more important to them.

Men, of course, like to believe that they are more often engaged in loftier or more sacred pursuits. To the women their secret *corroborees* are a central feature in their lives.

In some areas they are carried out with a certain degree of regularity, and are organized by the older women at the request of the younger. The men know about them, of course, but they are not certain of what takes place at them or what songs are sung. The secrecy apparently adds somewhat to the excitement and anticipation current at the time of these *corroborees.* The men certainly know that the women return from the ceremonies elated and excited.

The songs the women sing are highly erotic in character and usually describe, with a good deal of intimate detail, the situations or relationships the women wish to bring about. When the songs are sung, the magic of them is supposed to influence the men, who experience heightened sexual desire.

In at least one way the *corroborees* serve an important social function—to strengthen marital ties. Married women believe the songs and rituals will strengthen their husbands' desire for them.

But sometimes the magic becomes too strong—or the excitement too great—and what results is a rearrangement of partnerships and affiliations. Some women, particularly young women, a number of whom may be married to the one old man, get "new boys"—for there are usually numbers of young men in a tribe for whom there are no wives.

(Tjalkalieri's second wife, forced on him by tribal procedure, became an embarrassment to him since he lived near the mission. Polygamy is frowned on by missionaries, but there is no such moral censure in the tribal state.)

The *corroborees* thus often promote irregular relationships, but the women, although realizing some of the penalties for such social transgressions, believe themselves forearmed because of the essentially magical nature of the ceremonies.

There is no doubt that magic is believed to be the source of the changes that take place. Women with small babies rarely attend the rituals for fear the magic that they believe will enter them will pass to their children through their milk and poison them.

In aboriginal society men are often away from their wives for considerable periods, hunting or merely on walkabout. In these circumstances a woman, skeptical of her husband's fidelity, may carry out magical ceremonies to keep him faithful while he is away.

But the efficacy of such procedures is, of course, very much open to doubt. When a woman suspects that her husband or lover has not been faithful to her, she may, and often does, carry out vindictive sex magic against him.

One method is to "poison" herself in a series of rituals so that, she believes, his next contact with her will produce

venereal disease. This is a magical procedure that has undoubtedly developed since the coming of white men and is
associated with irregular unions with them.

Some of the charms worn by both sexes are believed to
exercise a great deal of power—and it is, of course, a selec-
tive power, picking out the particular person of the opposite
sex who is desired. Coastal natives wear shells that are
charmed. Lightning is sung into them, and it flashes and at-
tracts the desired person.

I asked the Pitjendadjara men about charms of this sort.
"The Aranda dogs make a *chilara*," said Tjalkalieri. "It is
a headband. They make it from possum or euro fur string.
The man puts power into it with a song and then he wears
it into the camp. The woman he wants sees him and her insides
shake with eagerness. At night she will creep into his camp."

There were murmurs of assent and one or two subdued
"*Yokais*" from the group.

There is a compulsive character about love magic. It is
a colorful and legitimate form of sexual selection and is, in
general, practiced by all adult tribal aborigines. It is carried
out by them as sedulously as romance and courtship are conducted in our own society, and as seriously as the mating
dances of the peacock and peahen.

Strangely, as the tribe breaks down, love magic diminishes
rapidly, although other forms of magic survive with much of
their tribal vigor.

Yungitcha gave me his little love-magic token and some
time later I showed it to Owen Anderson, a light-caste Queensland native who is thoroughly detribalized, but of Yuggrabool
tribal ancestry.

Owen immediately recognized the twirling stick as a love-
magic object.

"My people used to use such things a few years ago," he
explained. "Always these things had to be warmed over a
small fire made of the wood of a special tree. This fire gave

them 'life.' The fellow who was going to use it would do this, point the stick in the girl's direction, and then swing it on a piece of string and sing a special love song."

"What was the effect of this?" I asked Owen.

"It was only used when the girl could not be got through the proper tribal ways," he said.

"And after the man swung the stick and sang the song, what happened then?"

"Well, if he had done it all right, and good and strong, then the girl's mother and father felt something. They would get the girl and take her to the man."

"Do you know of any case like this that really happened?"

"I know what Bobby Logan told me. Bobby was working on Trewlawney Cattle Station some years back when a colored fellow called Willie Taldora from the Gulf country (Northern Australia) came to work on the station.

"This Willie Taldora went home with Bobby Logan one week end to Devon Creek, and he fell in love with Bobby's sister. After a while he saw the girl's people and said he wanted her.

"They said he couldn't have her because he came from long ways and was of different people. He said to Bobby Logan, 'I'll get that girl, you see!'

"Well, when they went back to work on the station this Taldora fellow said, 'I know clever things that'll get that girl for me,' and he made one of the twirler things, and he hotted it up over a fire and twisted it and sang a song in his own lingo.

"Bobby Logan told me this Taldora was a pretty wild blackfellow. I guess he was pretty clever, too.

"Next morning after he'd done this thing, he saw Bobby Logan and said, pretty cheeky like, 'You better watch out for your people to come. They gonna bring that girl to me.'"

I interrupted Owen to ask how far Trewlawney Station was from Devon Creek.

"Thirty miles it was. And that night, sure enough, Bobby Logan saw his people arrive with the girl, his sister. When they saw him they said, 'Where's that Willie Taldora fellow? We got the girl that he wanted, and we're going to give her to him.'

"They got married, sure enough."

"And you think it was twirling the stick and singing the song that did it, Owen?" I asked.

" 'Twasn't nothing else," he declared.

CHAPTER 9

Life with the Dead

"You gotta be careful when them *yunbin* are about," said Tom Kenny. "They might catch your *wogai*."

We were talking about ghosts—a favorite topic of conversation with aborigines—in this instance about the rather strange manifestations that might best be described as nature spirits. The aborigines believe in a world teeming with spirits, and *yunbin* (in the Gidabul dialect) are a type of these similar to fairies or gnomes. The *wogai* that Tom thought might be caught is a person's spirit.

There were about half a dozen natives in the group at Woodenbong, typical of the type of gathering we liked to arrange among detribalized natives for discussions of this sort.

There was Tom Kenny, nuggetty, about sixty years old, intensely sincere; Tom Close, a good deal older, querulous, and talkative; Harry Monsell, also an old man, but tough and muscular, unpretentious but impressive; small, frail old Danny Sambo, and a few others.

We were sitting on an open veranda at Woodenbong. The Woodenbong settlement is a sprawling government station for aborigines, tucked away in the northeast corner of New South Wales, just south of the ranges separating it from Queensland, and on the fringe of the rich coastal dairy country.

Woodenbong has a shifting population of from 150 to 200. Families come and go, moving from place to place on walkabout, a trait that has hardly diminished at all despite the acculturation of the aborigines. Tribes represented there come from as far south as Coff's Harbor (two hundred miles) and into Queensland. Although the tribes have long broken up as such, many of the tribal customs persist, and among all the old and most of the young the various dialects are spoken in addition to English.

It was just after dusk when our group gathered, and wraithlike mists were settling around the river flats. The blue spurs of the McPherson Ranges in the distance had melted into the purple of the night. The evening was chilly, and we gathered closely around the fire glowing in a makeshift brazier.

"Them fellows you were talking about, Tom," said Harry Monsell, "we call *mogwee*. I seen one of them. And it was right here at Woodenbong a few years ago. Oh, he was a big fellow—must have been nearly eight feet long—but he weighed hardly nothing at all. He used to swing about on the ends of horses' tails. They used to try and shake him off, but he used to laugh and laugh."

"What did he look like, Harry?" I asked. "I mean, was he like an aboriginal?"

"I suppose he was, 'cause he was sort of colored like, but you could see right through him most times, they say. It was just near dark when I seen him. I was riding along by the river flats and my pony got all excited, and when I looked back, there was this fellow hanging onto its tail and laughing and laughing."

"Could you hear him laughing?"

"I don't remembers now, but I could see him. And I did gallop!"

"They say there's a little red man about here, too," said Tom Kenny. "Nellie Charles said she seen him. He's about two feet high and red colored. Other people about Woodenbong seen him, too. Might be the fellow that belongs to Mount Lindesay comes down sometimes."

"Nellie Charles seen him last week," said Harry, "but the last time I seen him was about twelve or thirteen years ago—a little fellow and bright red."

Tom Close took off his steel-rimmed spectacles and, breathing heavily on the lenses before polishing them on his vest, he said, "Mostly you see these fellows about this time of night."

Some fearful glances attempted to penetrate the gloom around us.

"But," he reassured us, as he examined his spectacles against the glow of the fire, "usually they don't hurt you none. Mostly them folk belong to a mountain, or a creek, or a big boulder, and they tries to scare people that go near them. Now in the old time, if a fellow came here from Queensland way, he might be going along this time o' night and he'd see someone like that little red man. He'd be dead scared, all right, and he'd come along to us and say what he'd seen. 'Oh,' we'd say, 'you seen the little red man. He won't hurt you none.'"

"Do the clever-men have anything to do with these spirits?" I asked.

"I dunno," said Harry Monsell, "but one time up at Inkerman Station in Queensland [near Ayr], when I was about nineteen, some fellows got to having a *corroboree* and they brought some of these *mogwee* around.

"They was pretty wild blackfellows, four of them, and we all used to sleep in the one shed. I didn't know their *corroboreeing* songs, so I just watched them. After a while they lay down and went to sleep. I didn't go to sleep because I could hear a noise like a *goanna* [iguana] moving round the shed.

"I got up and struck matches, but I couldn't see nothing. As soon as I lay down, the noise started again. I tried to wake

the others up but I couldn't. Them *mogwee* must've put
them to sleep.

"After about two hours the noise stopped and I heard a
long whistle. Them *mogwee* often whistles. Then I could hear
paper being torn up—lots and lots of it. It was a quiet night,
just like tonight, and the noise of the tearing was pretty loud.

"Next morning I looked right round the shed and there
wasn't no paper nowhere."

There were murmurs round the group of *"mogwee," "yunbin"* or *"booyinyah,"* all meaning "ghost" in the variety of
dialects represented.

"Another time, too," Harry went on, "I was staying in a
shack at Woodhouse. It was a moonlight night, and I was
sleeping on the floor and could look through the open doorway. I heard the noise of someone walking round the shack.
The noise came round to the front of the shack and the footsteps came up the steps, across the veranda, and through the
doorway. I could see as plain as anything—and there wasn't
nothing there to go with the footsteps.

"Then whatever it was knocked a box of matches off the
table in the room. Next morning I looked about and I couldn't
see no footprints at all, not a man or animal."

"You bin pretty good at tracking, too," said Digger Marine, sitting in the gloom on the outside of the circle. At this
time Harry was, indeed, a police tracker and was, I heard
from several people, an unusually good one. Until just a few
years ago he was occasionally called on to search for people
lost in the wild country near the ranges.

Desert natives reported that stones or other objects were
sometimes mysteriously thrown at them. All these experiences are suggestive of poltergeist (mischievous spirit) phenomena, comparatively well known to western civilization, and
reported also to be common among other native peoples.
Typically, objects are thrown and a variety of inexplicable,
mischievous acts occur, apparently by unknown agency, and

these are almost invariably associated with an adolescent youngster, usually a girl.

But, while no clear-cut case for typically poltergeist phenomena was obtained, the aborigines gave evidence of belief in partly human, prankish nature spirits.

The aborigines also reported seeing ghosts; in fact half of those who answered our questionnaire said they had seen one. Here a pattern of similarity to western experience developed.

The story that Danny Sambo told that night is similar, in many respects, to reports of apparitions recorded by whites.

"A few years back, when I was camping by a creek at Wiangara," said Danny, "I seen a figure of a woman walking along by a fence. And as I watched her, so help me, I could see the fence through her. I knew it was a *wogai*, and I thought it was one that couldn't rest.

"I was new in them parts, and I said to the colored people near there next day, 'I seen a *wogai* last night.' They said, 'Was it down by the creek, near the slip rails?' and I said, 'Yes.' And they said, 'It was a colored girl, wasn't it?' and I said, 'Yes.' They said, 'That was a *wogai* you seen all right. That was Lena Brown's *wogai*. Her husband killed her about twenty years ago, down by the slip rails. Lots of folk seen Lena Brown.'"

There were murmurs from the others. This, indeed, was a "real" ghost.

Tom Close explained that when a native dies a violent death, his spirit lingers about the place, haunting it for, perhaps, years afterward. This is also a common western belief. Usually, Tom said, you see the ghosts of the dead for only a few days after the death, three or four at the outside. Then they disappear and are not heard of again.

That is why, in tribal organization, natives immediately move camp when a death occurs, for the haunting is believed to occur around the camp or residence of the deceased.

"Now, take that Naomi Holton girl," said Tom. "Her mother died some months ago, but the *wogai* still comes round and pesters her."

We had spoken to Naomi, a shy thirteen-year-old, about this only a short time before. She had been one of our subjects in a program of testing we were carrying out for the Commonwealth Office of Education on the educability of aborigines.

We had almost classed her as untestable, so shy was she. She was a pretty child, as aborigines go, but she kept her face hidden behind her hands, her big brown eyes just peeping out occasionally as she whispered, "I don't know," to each of our questions. We could at first find no bond of rapport.

But gradually, as we persisted, she weakened. The hands slipped a little lower, her voice was a little less timid. She used to look firmly at the ground and make aimless drawings with her toes in the dust, but she began to unfold, and we found her to be surprisingly bright.

After her mother's death Naomi had no home. Her big brother, Tom, moved off the station to work on a dairy farm, and she drifted for some months from cottage to cottage, family to family, on the settlement, unloved and uncared for. A little while later the Government named her an uncontrollable child, and Lyn and I were asked to take her into our home as a ward. Great though our affection was for the child by this time, we felt that it would be doing her a greater unkindness to take her completely away from her own people, comparatively neglected though she might be.

Naomi had told us how, nearly every night since the death of her mother, just as she was settling down to sleep, her mother appeared as a vision. The mother didn't seem ghostly, but appeared as she did when alive, and as she was usually dressed. Naomi told us she would speak to her mother, who seemed to be disturbed, asking her to go away and not to trouble her.

"That *wogai* might stay for months," said Tom.

Harry Monsell cut in. "I seen that Holton woman's *wogai* down by her house one night a few weeks back."

So the discussion went on. Inevitably it led to an inquiry into natives' ideas on personal survival. Strangely, these are rather confused. This essentially religious problem has received far less attention and is regarded as far less significant than most aspects of magic.

In the tribal state all deaths are regarded as having a magical cause (hence the importance of inquests by clevermen to determine the person responsible), and usually the spirit has passed to its future state, to the Dream Time whence it came, by the time the funeral rites are completed.

But the situation is confused somewhat by the concept of each native having a number of spirits. There is, for example, what might be termed the primary spirit or soul which existed before the birth of the native and at his death returns to the Dream Time, to totemic spirit groups, or to the god Baieme. There is also at least one secondary spirit, probably created by the magical cause of death, which is like a ghost. This survives usually for about three days, longer in the case of violent deaths, but then just disappears.

There is a belief, too, that the dead person might use his body again, so in some tribes relatives tie the hands of the corpse behind the back, or perhaps mutilate it by removing the eyes, and the mourners return to their new camp through a smoke screen so that they won't be followed.

The Dieri people in Central Australia, who bury their dead (some tribes have tree burials), carefully sweep a clear patch around the grave, and for months natives look there each evening or morning to see if there are any tracks. If there are, the body is moved to another grave since it is thought to be dissatisfied with the existing one.

The secondary spirit, or ghost, is apparently seen quite frequently by relatives and close friends. They speak to the apparition, calling on it to leave them in peace. When their invocations are in vain, a tribal clever-man may be called in to exorcise the spirit.

Some strange beliefs have developed around the fact of death. One, for example, is that a dying man becomes suddenly invested with clairvoyant ability of the most extraordinary sort. His last hours are thus likely to be filled by intense cross-examination on a wide variety of subjects. Even the sophisticated native believes that the one occasion during his life on which he can know the answer to any question is three days after his mother's death. He must stand at the foot of the grave and ask his question.

In some cases clever-men claim that they are able to maintain regular communication with the dead. They claim to be able to make spirits manifest themselves at certain special *corroborees* that very strikingly resemble spiritualist séances in our own society. In the Kurnai tribe an aboriginal mediumistic doctor was said to be carried aloft to the Dream Time with a whistling sound. A short time later the voices of spirits were heard. They answered questions about dead relatives, and predicted the future.

A curious feature of this man's performances was that in the morning following them he was found by tribesmen, still entranced, in odd locations and positions. One account states: "Finally, after all was over, the *birraak* [doctor] was found in the top of an almost inaccessible tree apparently asleep, where he said the *mrarts* [spirits] had left him when they went away." On another occasion he was found with a heavy log lying across his body.

To this particular tribe séances served two important practical purposes; the spirits manifesting at them told them of the movements of their enemies, and also when whales had been washed ashore, thus providing a bountiful food supply for them. The spirits, incidentally, claimed to be responsible for the stranding of the whales.

I told these stories to the group crouching around the embers dying in the brazier. The oldest ones among them, who could remember life in the tribe when they had been youths, confirmed that these were the sorts of things they had experienced.

We were silent for a while, and I noticed some of the natives looking into the darkness around us, contemplating the lonely return to their various camps. We all must have felt like the boy who whistled walking through a cemetery at night—we needed something to cheer us.

"I bin told off by a ghost," said Tom Kenny, breaking the silence.

"What, you been roused on by one of 'em!" exclaimed Danny Sambo, with an uncertain laugh. "So help me, I bet it was a woman ghost."

A ripple of relief passed round the circle.

"No, it was a man," said Tom, still serious. "My stepfather it was, and six months after he died."

"What did he say to you, Tom?" asked Digger Marine.

"Well, he didn't rightly speak to me, but he looked awful angry. If he could have spoke, he would have give it to me, all right."

"Tell us about it, Tom," I said.

"I was lying on a veranda one night, and I was on the lookout 'cause I was expecting a fellow called Archie Green to come and see me from down Tabulam way. I had my stepfather's dog with me. It was asleep at the foot of my camp.

"After a while that dog started to growl and its hair stood straight up. I couldn't see nothing at first. Then I seen a man coming along and I thought, 'Ah, here's Archie.' The dog was wagging its tail now, and it ran out and started to prance round this fellow.

"I got up, and I could see it coming towards me, and when it got closer I could see it was waving its arms pretty angry like and shaking its fists.

142

"Then I seen it wasn't Archie at all. It was my dead step-father. There he was coming towards me, angry as could be and making faces at me.

"I got ready to run, and then it disappeared and the dog started to howl."

"What did you do to your stepfather to make him so wild?" asked Digger.

"I didn't go to his funeral," replied Tom.

"So help me!" said Danny Sambo.

CHAPTER 10

Aboriginal Telepathy

Billie Combo was a Gidabul native of about fifty. After spending a few days under observation in the hospital at Kyogle, about forty miles from Woodenbong settlement, where many of his friends and relatives lived, he left and stayed with some aborigines in the township.

A few days after leaving the hospital he had a sudden heart attack and died. At the time of his death, as far as his people at Woodenbong knew, he was in reasonably good health.

Yet one of these people knew that he had died before news could have reached Woodenbong through ordinary channels, and at least two others had unusual experiences associated with his death.

First to tell us of his experience was Walter Page. He had had no clear-cut, unequivocal psychic knowledge of Combo's death, he said, but he had an unusual, disturbing feeling that subsequently he felt sure was associated with it.

Walter, an unusually intelligent native, one indeed who had represented his people as the aboriginal member of the Aborigines' Welfare Board, put it this way:

"I'm sure something happened to me when Billie Combo died, and I'm sure it was caused by his death. I was on the station here at Woodenbong that day. Suddenly I felt dopey—

144

it was as if a cloud came over my mind. I couldn't think; I was depressed and upset.

"When I went to lie down, my wife asked me what was wrong. I said, 'I don't know, but it's serious.' She said, 'Is it one of our people, Walter?' I said, 'No,' because if it had been one of our people, that is, someone related closely to us your way or by the totem, I would have seen my totem rooster I always see when one of us dies. The rooster is the one that tells me of such things.

"But I had this strange feeling just the same. I tried to find out. I asked myself who it could be, but I didn't know. Later that day my wife went into the township and they told her they'd just heard that Billie Combo died."

"Was Billie related to you at all?"

"He was a cousin, but he was not a totem relative."

Later in the day we heard a similar story from Rene Robinson. Lyn and I were carrying out some routine investigating following our questionnaire.

Rene was asked: "Would you know if a relative some distance away died, had an accident, or was seriously ill?" Then we went on to explain, "We don't mean knowing because of a letter or telegram or someone telling you, but by something else, like a feeling."

Unhesitatingly Rene replied, "Oh yes! That's often happened to me. Our people often know like that."

She watched Lyn and me carefully as we noted down the conversation. She was a half-caste aged something over seventy. But her eyes were keen and her faculties sharp. Normally she was a cheerful woman, but as we mentioned this subject her wrinkles deepened, her eyes became thoughtful, and she became downcast.

"Has this sort of thing happened to you, Rene?" Lyn asked.

"Oh yes. Great sorrows come on me. I can't do no work. I lie down and I think and think, and this feeling lays heavy on me.

"I got like that when Billie Combo died last week."

Tears came into her eyes. She pushed a wisp of gray hair back on her head, and sat down.

"It comes awful heavy, that feeling. When I had it last week, I knew one of my people was gone. It was a feeling full of death. All our people know it."

"Did you know at the time that it was Billie Combo who had died?"

"No. I didn't know till I was told—but when I had the feeling, the great sorrow, I knew it was one of my people, for sure."

We told Rene that earlier Walter Page had told us of a similar experience. We asked her if she knew of anyone else who had been affected.

"That Danny Sambo," she replied. "He came over to my house that morning, and when he saw me lying down he said, 'You got the feeling, too?' And I said, 'Yes.' He said, 'I know, it's that Billie Combo died.' I said, 'You bin told?' He said, 'I bin told by my black crow that tells me these things.'"

Danny Sambo confirmed her story. "These things often happen to my people. More in the old time, of course, but with Billie Combo, both him and me was crow totem, so I must know, see?"

The three incidents associated with Billie Combo's death thus ranged roughly from a vague feeling and depression to complete conviction. Such things happen to white people. Hundreds of cases, checked and cross-checked, verified and documented, have been recorded. It was these that led, at the turn of the century, to experimental work in telepathy which has culminated in refined laboratory-type techniques.

But with the aborigines the conviction associated with a so-called crisis case, a type of incident that appears to be far more common among them than with white people, is often so profound that it moves them to action. In his book, *The Australian Aborigines*, Professor A. P. Elkin testifies to the as-

surance of aborigines following the receipt of apparently telepathic information. "Many white people, who have known
their native employees well, give remarkable examples of the
aborigines' power for knowing what is happening at a distance,
even hundreds of miles away. A man may be away with his
employer on a big stock trip, and will suddenly announce one
day that his father is dead, that his wife has given birth to a
child, or that there is some trouble in his own country. He
is so sure of his facts that he would return at once if he could,
and the strange thing is, as these employers ascertained later,
the aborigine was quite correct; but how he could have known
they do not understand, for there was no means of communication whatever, and he had been away from his own people
for weeks and even months."

In our inquiry into the reality or otherwise of the psychic
phenomena underlying the magic of Australian aborigines, my
wife and I have been particularly impressed by one feature.
It is that the spontaneous experiences of ordinary aborigines
so closely resemble those of white people, bearing in mind
minor differences applicable because of the wide gap between the two cultures.

This, of course, is to be expected if the reported experiences of white people are genuine, and it is, indeed, collateral
evidence for them. The aboriginal case material shows, too,
that such experiences are modified or conditioned by their
culture, but that a basic pattern is present. In no aspect is the
pattern clearer than in instances of what is called "crisis telepathy" where the illness, danger, or death of a distant relative
or friend is involved.

Now, in typical crisis cases experienced by white people
there is almost invariably a strong emotional relationship between the two people concerned. This relationship presumably facilitates the telepathic link that seems to occur in a time
of crisis. Sometimes this is weak and may manifest itself as a
vague feeling; at other times it carries more conviction by

being "mediated" in some way. That is, the recipient sees a vision of the other person, or hears that person's voice, both seeming, for the moment, real; or he may have a particularly vivid dream giving the essence of the information. It would seem that such are psychological in nature, and are, to use the technical term now applied to them, "mediating vehicles."

Aborigines, too, have such mediating vehicles, and the interesting point is this: the more tribalized natives, such as Danny Sambo, have information mediated through a totemic animal or bird, while less naïve natives, like Frank Mitchell who knew of the death of his small son, Billie, gain the information by means very similar to those experienced by white people.

After we had discussed his experience at Billie Combo's death with Danny Sambo, the little old man went on to tell us of another experience he had had only two months before.

"I was staying with Harry Monsell at the time," he said. "Harry and me was sitting outside his place one night talking about the old times. It was early in the night, too, and the camp was noisy. Them Christians was in the hall singing away, in the hut next door they was having an argument, and just over the hill behind the water tank some dingoes was howling. But, over it all, so help me, I could hear my little old black crow crying out to me.

"I said to Harry, 'You hear that crow?' He listened a while and he said, 'Yes, I hear him.' And I said, 'That fellow's my *djurabeels*.' Now that fellow Harry Monsell's an old Birri fellow from right up Queensland way, but being old time hisself he could hear the crow of mine.

"He said to me, 'That crow tellin' you something?' I said, 'Yes, he bin tellin' me something all right, but there's too much noise. I think I'll go to bed and listen.'

"Well, I went to bed and, so help me, I could hear that crow cawing and cawing trying to tell me something about my peoples.

"Next day they told me Harry Little's wife died at Tabulam that night 'bout the time Harry Monsell and me did hear the crow. She got sick in the afternoon and they sent for old Fred Cowlin. Fred said she'd been caught by someone and he couldn't do nothing. He said she would die."

The mediating function of the totem is more pronounced in the case of natives who have once been tribal, for these natives believe that each is magically related to his totemic animal (*djurabeels* or *barmyunbaie* among the Woodenbong people) and that the members of the same totemic group have spiritual contact with each other through the totem.

Such beliefs may appear to be primitive indeed, but some natives have a surprising insight into the psychology of the totem in these experiences.

Walter Page, for example, gave Lyn and me a number of accounts illustrating the part his totem rooster played in crisis cases. "That bird is not real, I know," he said, when we questioned him on this point. "You see it with your mind."

Walter told us of an experience of his nephew, Earl Ferguson, who is an engine driver (railroad engineer).

"Earl was living at Coraki when this happened," Walter said. "He had gone to Walgett [N.S.W.] and he was sitting on the veranda of a hotel with three other fellows—white men. While they were sitting there he saw his *djurabeels*—that's his totem—that looks just like a rooster. This rooster was with other fowls in the yard. As Earl was watching it, it came away from the other fowls, right onto the veranda. Just then a waitress came along and shooed it away.

"Earl knew the bird was *djurabeels,* and he said to the other men, 'You fellows won't believe this, but I'm gonna get some bad news soon.' They said, 'How do you know?' and he told them about the rooster, which they couldn't see any more.

"They said, 'That's blackfellow talk. We don't believe such things.' Just then the waitress came back and she said, 'I've been told to find a dark fellow called Ferguson.'

" 'That's me,' said Earl. 'You got bad news?' She said, 'You're wanted long distance on the telephone.' Well, that telephone call was to tell Earl that his old grandmother had died. She took ill real sudden."

When we pointed out that he had said the waitress shooed a "mind" rooster away, Walter explained, "When those *djurabeels* come, oftentimes other folks see them, too. They don't know they're *djurabeels*, of course."

Bertie Mercy, a barrel-chested old man, a font of psychic lore, recounted an experience he had had a little while before. He and his wife, Beatrice, were sitting outside their shack one night when they both saw a plover flying overhead.

"That got me to thinking," said Bertie. "Beattie said to me, 'Something's up.' I said, 'Yes,' because I know the plover totem. Then I said, 'I think it's old uncle at Coff's Harbor. That plover come to tell us he died.' That was true, too. We found out that old uncle died that very night."

Coff's Harbor was two hundred miles distant.

Bert Mercy, too, thought the bird they had seen was not real, but an illusion.

On the other hand, Owen Anderson, a caste native far more sophisticated than Bert Mercy, and who had adapted himself to western ways far more satisfactorily than Walter Page, was convinced that his experiences with his totem, the water hen, involved a real bird.

"I've seen that bird," he declared, "and I know it was real. Why, I saw it only last week. Doreen and me was sitting outside the camp here at Churchill one night, and we both saw that water hen. It came flying right over the camp from down New South Wales way.

"Doreen said, 'Someone from Tabulam's sick or one of my people's coming to see me.' Next day her brother Christie came walkabout from Tabulam."

Apparitions sometimes take the place of the totemic vision or are associated with it. Alec Vesper, a Bundulung native

from Pretty Gully, gave this account. "Little whiles back at
Pretty Gully I was sitting down with some fellows—there
was Dick Piety, the preacher, and Sippy Doolan and some
others. It was a pretty still night, and all of a sudden there
was an awful bang on the roof, like it was a big stone come
down from long ways.

"I said to the others, 'By golly, something's wrong. Something's gonna happen by'n'by.'"

"Did you have any idea at the time what that might be?"
I asked.

"No," said Alec, "but I was pretty scared 'cause that sort
of thing had happened to me before, and every time there
was some bad news soon after.

"That night I couldn't sleep. I was restless, tossing and
turning about. And then I seen my sister, standing there by
the door, just like real. (She used to work in a town nearby.)
But I knew it was a vision I seen. She didn't say a word—just
stood there—and I knew she was dead.

"Next morning I said to Dick Piety, 'You know that stone
that fell on the roof? The bad news is gonna be about my
sister. She just died.' He said, 'Has it been revealed to you?'
and I told him about the vision. He got his Bible out and read
from it, 'And lo, a spirit passed before me, and the hair of my
flesh stood up.'

"Later that morning a telegram came. It said my sister had
took ill very sudden and died in the night."

"What do you think made the bang you heard?" we asked.

"I dunno," he said. "I guess it must be spirits or the Lord
Hisself.

"That Tom Kenny fellow hears bangs, too, they tell me."

Tom Kenny heard thumps, he said, not bangs. They were
caused by his *barmyunbaie*, who was a young man. This young
man would attract Tom's attention either by whistling or by
thumping the ground.

"When was the last time this happened to you, Tom?"

" 'Bout two year ago," he replied. "I was working near Kyogle chipping bananas when I heard these thumps on the ground. I stopped working and listened and the thumps came again, good and loud.

"I got to thinking, 'This must be my *barmyunbaie* fellow, and he's trying to tell me something,' but I couldn't figure out what it could be for a while. Then I said out loud, 'Hey, you *barmyunbaie*, listen to me. Is it my mother?' There was a real big thump then and I guessed it meant yes. So I packs up and goes straight into Kyogle to my mother.

"That *barmyunbaie* told me right, for sure. My mother had got sick, and I got there just before she died. She told me she wanted me to come."

Just as, to the tribal native, the totem is an appropriate mediating vehicle for information that is apparently acquired telepathically, so natives who have embraced Christianity find angels performing similar functions in their psychic experiences.

This was the case with Rene Robinson. She said that some years ago she was very ill in Coraki hospital. The white doctor attending her told her relatives there was no hope of recovery for her. Rene's relatives unwisely passed this information on to her.

"I was sick near to death that night, all right," she said. "Then I had a dream that gave me a great understanding. I dreamt I was floating through the clouds and some beautiful angel fellows came up to me. They looked real lovely. They said to me, 'Rene, you ain't gonna die. You got to live a while yet. You gonna get well.'

"I told that doctor fellow in the morning, too. And you know what?" she said, with delightful simplicity, "I didn't die neither—just like them angels said."

Dreams have always fascinated human beings. All cultures, including our own, have regarded them as sources of revelation, the means by which a person might glimpse, however uncertainly, into the future. Dream interpretation has flourished as one of the secret arts of magic, the dream interpreter a specially endowed individual able to find the true meaning behind the symbolisms and distortions. Dreams have been investigated both scientifically and unscientifically, by the cautious and by the credulous, and even now they hold almost as much mystery for us as they do for aborigines.

It does not seem unlikely that the dream state—that fringe of consciousness that is a condition of quiescent receptivity— is well suited to psychic impact. If we are indeed capable of experiencing telepathy, this is likely a favorable state.

To the aborigines, whose psychic nether world they give the name Dream Time, this is indeed so. And, as with us, clearcut, vivid dreams, dreams that are easily remembered, comparatively free from distortion, rich in detail, are those to which aborigines attach considerable importance.

In dreams, too, items of tribal, totemic, or family significance have their place. While the water hen had totemic significance to Doreen Anderson, her husband Owen attached great importance to unusual experiences associated with water and particularly to dreams in which water played a big part.

Owen recounted a number of what are termed veridical or "truth-telling" dreams. He accepted a cigarette and we sat down on the grass near his neat little cottage at Churchill.

"A few years back," he began, "I was working on a dairy near Beaudesert in Queensland. My eldest sister worked in the township. One night I dreamt I was standing by a deep pool of water. There was an aeroplane flying overhead but it wasn't making any noise. As I watched it, it suddenly nosedived into the water without making a splash or even a ripple.

"Then I started to dream all about the springs nearabouts Beaudesert. They were all flowing without stopping and soon there was a big flood. There was a fellow in the dream who worked with me at the dairy and soon the two of us were in water up to our chests. I said to this fellow, 'I think our time's up.'

"Then I woke up. The dream frightened me a lot because every time I dream of water something bad happens in my family, so I readied myself for bad news. I was pretty sure it was about my sister.

"I said to the fellow who worked with me, 'I dreamt about water last night. I think there's something wrong with my sister. I think she's pretty sick.'

"Well, they say dreams do tell true, and this one did. Later that morning a policeman from Beaudesert came out to the dairy and asked for me. When I saw him I said, 'You got bad news for me,' and he said, 'That's right. Your sister died at six o'clock this morning.'"

Owen tossed his cigarette end away and lay back contemplating the sky. "Only last year when I was working at Glenore Grove the same sort of thing happened to me. This time I dreamt of a flood, too. A great roaring flood of muddy water it was, with lots of logs floating in it.

"When I had this dream, I knew there was trouble again because of the water, and this time I thought of my people here at Churchill. Sure enough, I was right—a telegram came soon after to say my father was ill in Ipswich Hospital.

"Straightaway I went to Ipswich. My father was very sick. My brother and me took turns to sit by the bedside.

"Two nights later I dreamt I was standing by a pool. I dived into the water. It was very deep. I tried to get to the bottom, but no matter how hard I tried I couldn't reach it. Finally I had to come to the surface to breathe, and standing by the side of the pool, when I came up, was my father.

"I knew this was the end. Even in my dream I knew this. When I went to the hospital that day, I saw my brother. I said, 'I been dreaming again and it looks bad.' My brother said, 'Yes. He's gone to sleep and I don't think he'll wake up again.' My father died that day."

Knowledge of the death of another person who may be many miles away is, in both our own and aboriginal society, regarded as evidence (not conclusive, of course) for telepathy. It is the least farfetched of hypotheses to account for the coincidences.

This explanation can hardly be advanced for those cases, not common it is true, where the person accurately foretells his own death some time in advance. Perhaps there is a form of precognition, a subconscious foreknowledge of imminent death, perhaps even a willing to death.

One day I was talking to Tom Kenny about the strange death of the old fellow at Hermannsburg who apparently was aware of his own impending death.

"I know that's true," said Tom. "I seen that sort of thing long times ago in the tribe. There was an old fellow in my tribe name of Long Mick. He was a *wee-an* [doctor]. One day I seen this old fellow sitting down and bringing out all his clever things. The old men of the tribe were all round him.

"Long Mick was looking pretty careful at all his clever things—there was stones and teeth and charcoals and other clever things I hadn't seen before.

"I said to one old man, 'What's Long Mick doing that for?' He said, 'He's bin caught by enemy *wee-an.*' Another man said, 'That other *wee-an* come up in a storm and caught Long Mick.' Another one said, 'That doctor made the storm hisself to come up in.'

"Long Mick was moaning now. They said, 'That other enemy doctor must be pretty clever. Long Mick says his own clever things ain't clever enough. He says he's gonna die.'

"Well, Long Mick said that dinner in two days was the last meal he would have with them. And sure enough, just as the sun went down on that day, Long Mick died.

"Just before he died a white man name of Montgomery, who owned a station there, came to see Mick because he heard about what Long Mick said. Long Mick told him, 'I must die.'

"How could Long Mick know he was going to die?" I asked.

"Our people know more about such things than you white people," replied Tom Kenny. It was not a criticism of our culture's psychic obtuseness; it was a statement of fact as he saw it. The aborigines, it would seem, are indeed more keenly attuned to such subtle aspects of life and death.

The conditions favoring psychic awareness are probably optimum in the case of the aborigines. Certainly they do not inhibit such experiences. They have a social inheritance of belief in magic; their search for causal explanation has, indeed, barely progressed beyond recourse to mysticism and magic; they are often not merely ready to take note of and act on psychic hunches but, indeed, seek them.

On the other hand white people do not live in an atmosphere so highly charged. Their outlook is rationalistic and, unless a psychic impulse is of a truly impelling nature, tend to push it aside as irrational, or else it never comes to consciousness, but is lost in the welter of sensory experiences impinging on the individual.

In some instances with white people the psychic hunch comes to the surface in crisis cases, and it is in these that the elements common to the two cultures are clearly seen.

As the acculturation of the aborigines proceeds, and they adopt western ways of life and outlook, their psychic experiences diminish little and are not much reduced in intensity, but change in nature, losing tribal and magical significance and taking on characteristics more typical of the white pattern.

Immediately the question must come to mind as to whether, with their assimilation into the white community, the aborigines' sophistication will lead to a blunting of psychic awareness. Magic has impressed my wife and me as being that aspect of aboriginal culture which will survive when others disappear. We think that, while the aborigines retain their racial identity, their psychical experiences will be more frequent, more profound, and in general more reliable than ours.

CHAPTER 11

Sagacity and Superstition

"That," said Kinchika, "is good tucker." He had swung gracefully down from the little black pony, burrowed in the red earth with his bare hands, and produced a root or two of a type of nut grass. He chewed the tiny nodules appreciatively and then carefully repeated the name of the plant in his own language and in Aranda for our instruction, adding with a grin, "Plenty good tucker."

Tjalkalieri and I, our horses plodding along side by side, had been talking about food taboos applicable to his own and neighboring tribes. I was interested in the fact that there were magical penalties for violation of the taboos.

In the Aranda I found, for example, that youngsters who had not been initiated (and this applied equally to girls as to boys, for girls have a sort of initiation ceremony) are forbidden to eat quite a wide range of foods. If the taboo relating to any one is violated, it carries its own characteristic penalty. For example, if a boy eats wild turkey or wild turkey eggs, he is punished with premature senility, if he eats emu fat he will have abnormal sexual development; if a girl eats large quail or its eggs she is punished by her breasts failing to develop attractively, if at all, and so on.

Kinchika's definition of "good tucker" applied to items of food that were edible and available to him.

Many of the long hours traveling about Central Australia with this tiny nomad and Tjalkalieri for companions were spent in learning bushcraft in just the way that aboriginal youngsters do.

Good tucker and poisonous plants were carefully identified, the tracks of animals pointed out and explained, the stories associated with natural features discussed. The natives took a good deal of pleasure in teaching us their language in this way. They were overjoyed when we showed ourselves good pupils, roared with amusement when we incorrectly named a plant or animal, or mistook the mark of a euro's tail in the sand for the track of a snake.

As our Pitjendadjara vocabulary grew, Lyn and I were gradually able to increase the range of our discussions with these desert people. But abstract ideas were always difficult, and at first there were many occasions when language barriers stopped our inquiries. Tjalkalieri's expressive use of his own language, it must be said, was quite exceptional. Where I could translate it with little difficulty, it was poetic in nature.

During a halt in a trip one day I tried to ask Tjalkalieri if there was any one magical practice that was invariably successful. The halt was delayed for half an hour, an hour, as I tried to get the idea across. Eventually we got moving again, and I was prepared to give up all hope of having the question answered.

But Tjalkalieri persisted. He would ride up to me time and time again and say, "Boss. Is it like this?" suggesting his interpretation with a story or a description.

Late in the afternoon he was riding about a hundred yards in front of me when I heard a loud, excited *"Yokai!"* He swung his pony round and galloped the tired beast back to me.

"Boss," he said. "You listen. Right this time."

We dismounted and led our horses to the sparse shade of a desert oak as Kinchika and Lyn plodded up to join us.

Tjalkalieri was excited. He had, he thought, solved a problem—a problem of communication, anyhow.

"Like this, boss," he said, speaking almost entirely in English, which was unusual for him. "Doctor do something, always right, no gammon fellow. Right? Like this.

"Sometimes sun high in sky get dark; bad spirits make him dirty. [Although he referred to the sun as "him" it is regarded by aborigines generally as female, while the moon is male.] Light go 'way. Sun all the time dirty."

It took me some time to realize that Tjalkalieri was describing an eclipse of the sun. When I understood, he went on.

"All right. Doctor fellow come out, see bad spirits. Doctor take out clever-stones and chuck 'em at sun. Frighten bad spirits away. Okay? Always right. Clean up sun good-oh. Pretty clever, eh?"

Tjalkalieri had indeed illustrated the point I had in mind very prettily. Here was a piece of magic that was quite unlike bone pointing, love magic, rain making, which were not always successful; here was a piece of magic, comparatively rare in occurrence, of course, that had never been known to fail!

Was this practice magic, though, or was it plain superstition? There is an easy and almost imperceptible transition from magic to superstition, and the cutoff point depends on how rigidly we care to define one or the other. Magical beliefs and practices are frequently unusual and often grotesque, but there is a sameness, a pattern in them that runs consistently through the length and breadth of aboriginal Australia and has links with common human experience. On the other hand some queer beliefs are not common to a great many tribes. Often they are very localized. These are mostly superstitions.

Both magic and superstition arise from confused thought on cause and effect. In the case of the eclipse, for example, the sun invariably was uncovered following the clever-men's throwing of their stones, and the ritual had been assumed to be a causal one. Both magic and superstition are attempts to explain phenomena, to come to grips with reality. While it may be that, psychologically, superstition meets the needs of despair and magic those of credulous optimism, they are two attitudes that can, and frequently do, exist together; and neither is dependent on, or necessarily originates from, the other.

Frequently there is a superstitious element in magical practices, and the magic is obscured or distorted. Such occurs, for example, in many aspects of magic where it is believed that for the magic to be effective the song or chant that goes with it must be recited word perfect. Thus, while it may be true that in love magic deep desire and the tension associated with the ritual might well give rise to a sort of telepathy that makes the magic work, the word perfection of a chant is a superstitious addition.

Similarly, one of the great dangers associated with bone-pointing rituals is that the magic might backfire if there is any fault in the traditional procedure.

Magical beliefs associated with venereal diseases are obviously developments following culture contact with whites. There are others. For example, the Kaitish, a desert tribe living several hundred miles to the north of the Aranda, developed a form of sorcery that early investigators associated with the poison strychnine.

A native wishing to practice black magic against another sings power into an anthill. A portion of this he brings back to the camp where he carefully powders it and adds red ocher. At an opportune moment he scatters the powder about his enemy's camp. When the man lies down on it, the magic is thought to enter his body. In a few days he breaks out in sores, and later dies.

Normally red ocher is regarded as a life-giving substance —a film of it covers nearly all the possessions of desert natives except their spears and shields—but in this case is used in imitation of the red coloring matter added to commercial strychnine to identify it.

Tjalkalieri had hit upon a good example of magic that was always successful. There were some others that he might well have mentioned—we had only a few days before discussed how the *churinga* of the Jerboa rat, a marsupial with long whiskers, was rubbed on the faces of pubescent Aranda youths to induce facial hair growth.

Similar ceremonies are carried out with developing girls to bring about the growth of their breasts. At the appropriate time their nipples are painted with red ocher and with these two central points circles or spirals are drawn in clay, radiating outward. From time to time the drawings are renewed until the girls' breasts have reached a satisfactory size and shape.

In each case the rituals are believed to be the factors promoting the growth.

During our talks Tjalkalieri sometimes mentioned varieties of restrictions that applied to himself, or to Kinchika, to his totemic group, the tiger cat, or to the tribe.

The institution of taboos is something in which it might be supposed there is little reason. Taboos arise in two main ways—from superstitious beliefs and by decree of authority.

In the first way, improperly relating cause and effect is the usual source of trouble; if a native falls ill or has an accident, he may review his behavior for that day seeking a cause. He may realize that he has been in country he has previously not entered, drunk from a stream where he has never before quenched his thirst, or touched a rock he has not previously touched. He looks for the one different factor that might have affected him.

Thus there has developed a series of taboos associated with death-dealing rocks, dysentery-producing streams, and so on. Sometimes, of course, the native might be right in his conjectures. Far more often he is wrong.

Then taboos are often instituted for purely social reasons by tribal elders; men's meeting places are taboo to women and children.

Some taboos, mistaken though they may be in themselves, lead to eminently practical consequences. Restrictions placed on marriage between people related in a certain way are genetically sound. So, sometimes, are the reasons given for them, as I found when I questioned Tjalkalieri on this particular aspect.

"Keep the blood clean," he said. "Make good children, strong, good hunters—like me!"

One custom, the knocking out of one front tooth at about adolescence is, in the Aranda and Pitjendadjara, strangely associated with rain making. Almost invariably the two ceremonies follow closely one upon the other, and I asked Tjalkalieri about this.

He could give no sound reason but said, "Now face look like rain cloud." Presumably a once existing reason has now been obscured.

The actual procedure of tooth evulsion in his own case Tjalkalieri described with much humor and constant rib-poking of young Kinchika, who had yet to undergo the painful ordeal.

"All doctor come along when Tjalkalieri fixed up," he began. "Fill up mouth with fur cord to suck up blood. Then doctor come along and yank him out."

He illustrated this business of "yanking him out" on the unhappy Kinchika. He placed his lower teeth under and behind the lad's front teeth and imitated a sharp, upward jerk that, if he had been serious, probably would have brought with it, or at least loosened, the boy's front teeth.

"Then take *woomera* and knock, knock, knock 'im out. Then Tjalkalieri fixed up good-oh. All doctors cry out, 'Wah, wah, wah!' Pretty good, eh?"

After a moment's silence my friend began to laugh.

"Ha, that Maleiaba. He tell me, time come for him to be fixed up. Okay. Doctor bite, tooth not come. Doctor go knock, knock, knock, tooth not come. Okay. Do him again. No good. *Eecha, eecha, eecha!*"

(*Eecha* is a useful word, Aranda in origin, meaning "nothing," "failure," "broken," and so on.)

"*Eecha, eecha, eecha,*" emphasized Tjalkalieri, giggling.

"That doctor fellow said to Maleiaba, 'This fellow too much play about along girls.' Then the doctor took clay and gammon [pretends] to make Maleiaba's breasts like young girl. That fellow Maleiaba cried out, 'That's not true talk. You yank him out proper.'

"That doctor fellow tried again, and this time got the tooth out proper. My word, Maleiaba pretty pleased."

We unsaddled the horses and, while Kinchika gathered some wood for a fire and Lyn prepared a meal, Tjalkalieri and I went on to talk about another strange practice which probably arose from cannibalism, now infrequently heard of. The basic belief, that consuming a portion of a great warrior will lead to his qualities being acquired, is a very widespread one.

Ritual eating of a dead man is one way of obtaining spiritual nourishment. Some Central Australian people, when a great man dies, place his body on a tree platform and, as the body decays, young men stand beneath the platform and rub the juices that drip down into themselves. Similarly it is believed that the kidney fat of enemy warriors rubbed into weapons gives the owner strength and courage.

Tjalkalieri's account led me to recall one of the most barbarous acts attributed to aborigines. It was recorded by Dr. A. W. Howitt. His informant, Jupagalk, who was "very intelligent," told him: "When I was a boy I went out one day with some men to hunt. We were all walking in a line, when one of them hit the man in front of him on the back of the neck and knocked him down. Two or three of the men held me tight so that I could not run away, for I was very frightened.

Then the man cut open the one he had knocked down, by a little hole in his side below his ribs, and took out his fat. After that he bit the two edges of the cut together, and sang to make them join, but he could not succeed. He then said he could not do this because some one had already taken this man's fat before, as he could see by the marks on the liver, and that whenever a man had been opened, and closed up, no one could do it again. As they could not wake the man up, they buried him. They smoked the fat over a fire and took it away wrapped up tightly in a cloth. They wanted it to carry with them to make them lucky in hunting."

One is inclined to wonder if, in this instance, the native who carried out the operation did so in the belief that he would be able to close the wound and restore his victim in the same way as clever-men are supposed to do, but actually of course do not, when they carry out a magical operation to steal a man's kidney fat.

In the magical atmosphere surrounding the aborigines, it is believed that human behavior, death and disease, are, in some measure, controllable by human effort. There is no individual stagnation; everyone must play his part in directing the vital forces about him. When a man tries to play a part for which he is not fitted by training, however, it can lead to tragedy.

Tjalkalieri told me that when natives go on fat-stealing expeditions, they acquire fantastic magical powers. Such powers include the ability to change into animals (a magical idea strangely reminiscent of werewolfery), or tree stumps, or make themselves invisible. To evade the enemy a fat-stealer could put himself into a snake or lizard and escape, or became part of the natural landscape.

This last thought is consistent with the aboriginal Dream Time mythology and expresses their concept of their oneness with nature. All natural features in tribal territory are explained by Dream Time stories. This mythology from which their magic and superstition stem and by which they are regulated explains the origin and characteristics of these things.

One such myth decribes the travels of a Central Australian native in the Dream Time. During a hunt for a kangaroo he encountered a classificatory relative with whom he could not normally have intercourse. He violated and then killed her. This portion of the myth explains and illustrates a sexual prohibition. The native later threw down the skin of the kangaroo which became Lake Eyre, and he and his possessions turned into stone. This explains natural features; the native, his knife, and his bag can be seen today as groups of stones.

Strangely, aboriginal myths do not concern themselves to any extent with catastrophes and natural disasters such as floods, nor very much with violent aspects such as thunder and lightning. The emphasis in all phases of mythology and magic is usually on the normal and the commonplace.

While Tjalkalieri and I were talking about the magical acquisition of a dead man's qualities, he mentioned again the use of special *churingas* rubbed, usually on children, to produce certain effects. The *churinga* of the lizard totem, an animal whose flashing tongue might suggest verbal ability, is rubbed on tiny infants' lips to encourage early speech. Objects other than *churingas* are sometimes used; youngsters of about Kinchika's age try to get the leg bones of an eagle hawk to rub against their calves to encourage muscular development.

In a similar way charms are worn to protect natives against special perils, and verses are recited when natives go near an area of supposed magical potency.

Lady Luck is wooed by the desert natives and also by detribalized caste natives. Gambling, in fact, is a western weakness that aborigines readily embrace, and with it they take the white man's superstitions of "runs of luck," the use of good luck charms and rituals, and add a good many of their own. Even among sophisticated natives it is, however, not merely bad luck for the shadow of a menstruating woman to fall upon food, it is believed that poison is thus actually injected into it.

Luck implies an impassive attitude. Aborigines go a step farther and, with magical practices, attempt to influence the invisible psychic world around them; so that, while there is a superstitious element in much aboriginal magic, there is correspondingly a magical element in much aboriginal superstition.

Although he would joke about most aspects of his people's magical ideas, even bone pointing, there was one aspect that Tjalkalieri always discussed with the utmost gravity, although on the face of it, it was a wildly improbable notion. This was the belief, widely held, that doctors could travel vast distances in a short time with the aid of their magic cords.

Frequently he mentioned that Winjin or some other cleverman he knew could perform such miracles. Often on a journey he would say, "We take two day, three day, but that Winjin fellow, he can travel in no time."

Similarly coastal natives believed in this ability to travel fast that so closely resembles the claims of Yogi of Tibet. There is evidence, too, that in a sort of trance state a native might become aware of events at a distance as though he had actually traveled there. Technically this is known as "traveling clairvoyance." There is no doubt that natives believe they actually experience this.

Old Fred Cowlin told me he could travel thus from northern New South Wales to Brisbane. He could not, however, travel to Sydney. He said it was too far.

The son of a clever-man told me he had seen his father go to a creek, take off his clothes, and disappear. When he reappeared, only a few minutes later, he would claim to have traveled some hundreds of miles, and would give an account of what he had seen, which was often confirmed later.

Harry Monsell told me that when he was working as a cane cutter near Ayr in Queensland, there was a doctor who could regularly travel in a clever way.

"This fellow's name was Major," said Harry. "He used to work on the cane fields with us. Every Saturday when we knocked off work, me and my mates would go straightaway into the town, about four miles away. When we'd get there Major would always be there before us. Sometimes he left after us. No matter how fast we went, he always got there first.

"He couldn't go no other way but the way we went. He couldn't travel through the cane. We said to that fellow, 'How do you get here so quick?' and he said, 'I got clever things. They carry me here.'

"I heard about another fellow, too," continued Harry. "He made some uncles of Walter Page travel fast one day.

"It was near Grafton and these two fellows borrowed a gun from a fellow called Peter Fields, who was clever. The three of them went to Considine's Scrub, about three or four mile away, to shoot flying foxes.

"After they shot a few, this Peter Fields fellow said, 'We gotta be careful. There's enemy doctors flying around these parts. They might try to catch us. I better take you back to camp pretty quick. I better take you on that cord of mine that's clever.'

"Then he told them to sit down on a log. Well, those two boys sat down, and although it was daytime, they fell right off to sleep. Them doctors can make 'em go to sleep.

"When they woke up again, they were right back at the camp again. When they looked at the sun, they knew no time had gone by.

"A little while later Peter Fields come up to them and they said, 'How did we get here?'

"Peter Fields said, 'I done it with the cord like I told I would. I put you to sleep and brought you here.'"

Was it hypnotism?

Evidence we collected later strongly suggested it was.

CHAPTER 12

Hypnotism

Hypnotism can be invoked to explain many aspects of aboriginal magic, including fast traveling. By doing so, however, we place extraordinarily heavy demands on it and some explanations seem rather farfetched.

To explain the Major episode, for instance, we would have to assume that Major had hypnotized all his workmates, probably without their knowledge, and suggested to them either that they would see him in the township as an hallucination or that seeing him in the flesh they would have the impression that he had reached the township well before them. As a hypnotic procedure it would be complicated, a form of posthypnotic suggestion, and thus would be likely to break down.

But hypnotism is capable of producing some extraordinary effects, and any difference between the hypnotism we know and the hypnotism that may be practiced by aborigines may not be in kind but merely in degree.

Anthropological accounts, we found, made vague reference to the possibility of hypnotism among aborigines, recognizing them to be a very suggestible people, but nowhere could we find a statement that hypnotism was in fact used and that as a result certain effects were produced. And before invoking hypnotism to explain some aspects of magic, it would be necessary to show that aborigines are readily hypnotized and that hypnotism is practiced.

One of the aspects we had constantly to bear in mind was that if hypnotism were to be invoked to explain such phenomena as the magic cord and other aspects of the displays that clever-men give at initiation time, then mass hypnotism would probably be involved.

Mass hypnotism is a little understood and much abused term. If an operator takes a large group of subjects who have never before been hypnotized, there will be gradations of success. Roughly a fifth will fall readily into a deep trance state, others will be more difficult, while a few might be completely impervious to suggestion. But there is no question that two and more subjects can be hypnotized at the same time by a skilled operator, and if they have all been entranced previously as individuals or small groups, it is a relatively simple matter to induce collective responses including hallucinations.

Hypnotism, moreover, is extremely contagious. It is far easier to entrance a person who has previously seen another hypnotized, and where all in a group are predisposed to become entranced, the task of a skilled aboriginal clever-man would not be too great.

First, however, some facts on whether or not hypnotism was practiced had to be gathered. Once the problem had been resolved into simple terms, evidence, often of a conclusive nature, began to amass.

"Have you ever seen a doctor, or anyone else, put someone to sleep?" was soon a standard question Lyn and I were asking.

Walter Green, a handy man at Woodenbong, was emphatic in his reply. "Oh, yes! I seen Fred Cowlin do that oftentimes. He did that with my cousin, 'Erkie' Green, when 'Erkie' had the shakes.

" 'Erkie' was as sick as anything. He was shaking away and nobody could stop him. We sent for old Fred. Fred got out his very savage stone and he put it in the fork of a little branch and he stuck this branch in the ground.

"Then he told 'Erkie' to look at the clever-stone. He said he would get tired and go to sleep. Sure enough, 'Erkie' went to sleep. Old Fred lifted up 'Erkie's' arm—the shaking had stopped—and when he let it go, it fell down flop just like 'Erkie' was dead.

"Then old Fred said, 'Listen to me. That clever-stone of mine's got into you to make you better. You ain't gonna shake no more, "Erkie."'

"Later on he woke 'Erkie' up, and that fellow was cured all right. He didn't have shakes ever no more."

Peter Briggs, too, told us he had seen Cowlin put a man to sleep to cure him.

"'Bout a year ago at Tabulam there was a fellow called Jacky Ross," said Briggs. "One day Jacky said to me, 'I feel awful sick. I know a fellow who said he'd point me, and I bet he's done it.'

"I said to him, 'Is the fellow what done it clever?' and Jacky said, 'He must be clever. I feel sick near to dying. You better get that Cowlin fellow.'

"When old Fred come along, he looked at Jacky and he said, 'Jacky, you look at me. You ain't gonna die; you just gonna go to sleep. When you wake up you gonna feel real better.'

"He put Jacky to sleep, and he blew in his face and said to him, 'That fellow weren't clever, Jacky. You ain't bin pointed. You gonna live all right.'

"When Jacky woke up he said, 'By golly, that fellow couldn't have been clever at all. I feels real better.'"

This was exciting information.

Other natives gave accounts that suggested that hypnotism was far more widespread than we had suspected. Once the question had been properly put, the responses had meaning. Walter Page told us that years ago an old fellow named

Monty Robinson, who was supposed to be a doctor, cured him of persistent headaches. Monty would massage his head, blow into his ears and, looking closely into his eyes, tell him that his aches would stop, that he would go to sleep, sleep well, and wake up completely refreshed.

Bert Mercy said, yes, he had often in the old days seen doctors cure patients by sending them to sleep. There was a word in his tongue to describe this—*kulnarla.*

Joe Culham said that many years ago in Beaudesert (Queensland) he had often seen clever-men put others to sleep. Sometimes they would merely sing a special song; more usually, however, they used their clever-stones as well.

"Them clever-stones was real pretty," continued Joe. "Some of them was tiny and bright, just like diamonds. There was some big ones I seen, too.

"You know, them stones was real clever. I seen a doctor put one of them on a table. Then he spoke to it and it moved about, like it was alive. That stone could go different places and find things out for the doctor.

"That's what I seen him use to put fellows to sleep. They call this puttin' to sleep *tjingun* in my lingo."

Old Rene Robinson said she had heard of doctors putting people to sleep. "They use words that must be pretty clever. It's just like chloroform." She went on to say that she had heard of doctors stopping dogs from barking with the use of these powers, and it was this sort of thing that a clever-man did when he made kangaroos go "silly" on the hunt.

Tom Close told me that he had seen a native who had broken his leg badly—the bone was protruding—made to sleep by a doctor, who showed him a clever-stone, while the doctor set the leg. Tom said, too, that he had seen a *corroboree* at which a doctor had put about half a dozen natives to sleep. He was only a lad at the time and was not supposed to be watching the proceedings.

"I seen that Dick Piety put plenty of people to sleep," declared Eileen Mitchell. "Why, only last week down in the missionaries' hall he had 'em all lying about. His wife had to go round afterwards and slap their faces to make 'em wake up. He said it was the Holy Spirit what entered 'em, but me, I reckon it was hypnotism all right!"

Of the clever-men mentioned by these people, Fred Cowlin was the only one known to be still living. Fred was then camping at Tabulam, and we decided to visit him again. Tabulam, a tiny township on the Upper Clarence River, in the heart of the New England, was an ideal spot for inquiries about magic.

In the dilapidated government settlement on the banks of the river (a new settlement with modern fibro cottages has since been established), were Mumbi and Fred, two old men, both full bloods and initiates, who had lived with the tribe and were generally held to be clever. There was Robin Walker, last of the Upper Clarence natives to be initiated, who worked on a dairy just out of the township. He showed us the site of his initiation and told us how he had seen clever-men climb to treetop height with their magic cords. He showed us the sacred *bool* or ceremonial ring on the heights of Dingo Knob, the *wandarell* or play *corroboree* grounds where the whole tribe gathered for certain ceremonies.

Living in a humpy on the river bank was Susan Walker, a fine old full blood, raising two attractive teen-age granddaughters strictly according to old tribal precepts, herself a fountain of ancient lore.

Fred readily showed me his magic stone and demonstrated how he used it to "send fellows to sleep." Green had said he used it in a tree fork stuck in the ground. Fred also held it slightly above his subject's eye level. This is a practice used by white hypnotists; employing a small, bright light such as provided by an ophthalmoscope, or some other similar object, as a focal point for their subject's eyes, they hold it in this position, which is slightly tiring and tends to encourage sleep.

He told me of the song he sometimes sang to help the sleep come. It was like the song sung by "Brandy" in his magic-cord demonstration. A monotonous chant, the words were to the effect that "the doctor and his stone will take me to the Dream Time."

This was the first clear evidence of hypnotism being used by aborigines. When we came to discuss it in some detail, Fred expressed surprise that white people knew of it. He regarded it as very much a part of his magic and peculiar to it.

What did he use it for, apart from cures?

Fred outlined the training prior to initiation of young lads in his tribe many years ago. They were hypnotized, it seems, and sent on psychic journeys. As their training extended, they were taught to induce a trance in themselves, and while in this trance state to become oblivious to pain.

This tied in neatly with accounts of initiation ceremonies obtained by white men, including those given me by Tjalka-lieri. The postulants are instructed to gaze into crystals or a magic fire while a monotonous chant goes on. This chant is supposed to induce a magical sleep which is unlike ordinary sleep because the boys awake from it as men. The postulants behave in an apparently automatic way and their eyes seem glazed.

The physical trials that follow include the cutting of cicatrices, subincision, or circumcision, and ordeal by fire. Circumcision, Tjalkalieri told me, was, in the olden days, performed with a stone knife. In recent years the practice has been modernized somewhat and now, when it is obtainable, a razor blade is used. Fire ordeals were usually of the type just undergone by Kinchika, now in the first stages of his initiation.

The boy's arms bore many circular scars. They were caused by dry, pithy twigs being stood on his arm and lighted at the upper end. They burned down into the flesh, and he was required not to flinch or show any sign of pain.

When the Aranda were intact as a tribe, the series of rituals, trials, and demonstrations of initiation culminated in the postulants lying on a fire. Spencer and Gillen witnessed such a ceremony. The log fire was about nine feet in diameter, and the novices were required to lie on smoking boughs, although they did not come in contact with the red-hot embers.

After the boys had been on the fire once, for a period of about five minutes, the old men decided they must go on again. The fire was built up once more and the young men put on. One of the old men lifted the boughs at one side with a long pole to ensure that the fire smoldered.

Spencer and Gillen said there was no doubt of the trying nature of the ordeal. They knelt on the smoking boughs to see what it was like, but got up again "as quickly as possible." They were of course protected by clothes, whereas the natives were not.

The day on which this ceremony was recorded was hot—the temperature was 110.5 degrees in the shade and 156 degrees in the sun!

Cecil Taylor told us he had seen natives lying in a fire. "They were rolling about in it, scattering the fire everywheres. One old fellow was crying out, 'Wha, wha!' He seemed to be enjoying hisself. You know, them fellows never seem to get burnt."

Robin Walker said that he had been required to roll in a fire during his initiation. "It was hot," he said, with a grin, "but I didn't get hurt none. Them old fellows said it wouldn't hurt us none."

Fire walking among primitive peoples has been investigated by numbers of experimenters but we still are as far from a satisfactory explanation as we ever were. The temperature of fires braved by aborigines seems, in general, to be much less than that of the hot stones or charcoals walked over by Hindu or Island fire walkers.

Among Australian aborigines physical trials, it would seem, are not so much trials by pain but tests of the degree to which

174

the boys, as a result of previous instruction and practice, can hypnotize themselves and free themselves from pain.

This being so, an important point arises. Novices who fail initiation tests do not survive; so in the tribal state all initiates have been hypnotized deeply and are thus predisposed to subsequent hypnotic influence. In a way, a selection of the most suggestible occurs. Hypnotism therefore becomes of paramount importance in any discussion of aboriginal magic.

Owen Anderson had said he had seen Fred himself on a number of occasions in a self-induced trance. On one instance he mentioned in particular he had found Fred seated at the base of a gum tree. His eyes were open and turned upward. Owen, not at first realizing that the old man was entranced, tried to wake him. He said the clever-fellow felt limp, as if he were drunk. He was completely relaxed. Owen could not rouse him. When Fred recovered a short time later, he told Owen his spirit dogs had taken him on a journey.

Almost all discussions with aborigines on hypnotism evoked an account of hypnotism at a distance, or what might be called telepathic hypnotism. Natives have claimed that they could influence another man who might be half a mile or more away to do their bidding.

King Williams, for example, said his grandfather had hypnotized a native from a distance and killed him.

"In the old days my grandfather was very clever," said King. "He was so clever that a Queensland doctor was trying to catch him and kill him to show he was cleverer. My grandfather thought he had better catch this other fellow first. He couldn't get close enough to him ordinarywise, so he sat down and sang a song that made this Queensland fellow come to him.

"This was at Boonah, near the border. When this other fellow came up my grandfather said, 'I made you come. You bin trying to catch me.' Then he killed this fellow."

Bert Mercy recounted how his uncle stole something from a clever-man at Cedar Scrub, near Grafton.

"I was working with Uncle pulling potatoes when all of a sudden my uncle said, 'I don't feel good. Some fellow's watching us.' After a while he said, 'I got to lie down. Someone's doing something to me.'

"My uncle lay down and I went on working. Then I saw a fellow come into the paddock. He walked up to my uncle. 'This fellow pinched a thing belonging to me,' he said. 'I've come to get it. I made him like this so I could get it.'

"This fellow took something from my uncle's coat. Then he said to me, 'He'll wake up soon. You tell him not to pinch things.'

"When my uncle woke up, I told him what had happened. 'I should have knowed not to take anything from a doctor fellow,' he said."

Old Susan Walker said she had seen a doctor do the same sort of thing when she was a girl.

"This doctor fellow, name of Fred Ferguson, said to me one day, 'You see that fellow over there? I'm gonna make him come across to me.'

"Being only a girl then, I figured this Fred Ferguson fellow was trying to show off, and I didn't believe him. 'You watch him,' he said.

"Well, he sat down and gave a sort of a groan, and I thought he was sick. Just then the other fellow, who was walking along on a path, stopped. He looked round. Then he started to walk over towards our camp. I felt real queer.

"When he came to the camp, he walked right up to Fred Ferguson and he said, 'I felt you call me.' Fred said, 'That's right. I made you come here. I got clever-things like this 'ere stone to bring you.'

"That was long times ago, but I remembers it clear as it was yesterday," concluded Susan. "Them doctors and their stones was awful clever."

It is not surprising that, since quartz crystals and other unusual-shaped stones are used directly for hypnotism, na-

176

tives have assumed that great power resides in the stones.

Owen Anderson told me that one day a few years back he was digging a garden over an old aboriginal camping ground near Devon Creek. There he discovered a stone that impressed him because of its regular shape. It was brown, rounded, and felt very heavy. Clarrie Walker, who was working on the farm with him, said it looked like a clever-stone.

"I put that stone in my pocket," declared Owen, "and forgot about it. Wasn't till some months later when I was at Baryulgil I began to feel queer. I felt so queer I decided to go to Tabulam to see old Fred Cowlin.

"As soon as I seen Fred, he said to me, 'You got something clever with you,' and then I remembered the stone. I gave the stone to Fred. He said, 'That's a clever-stone all right. One time that belonged to a clever-fellow. He's dead now, but that stone's still alive. I better kill it before it hurts someone.'

"As soon as Fred took the stone away, I felt all right again."

Another native was interviewed while on leave from a mental hospital where he was being treated for paranoiac schizophrenia. He claimed that he had been sent mad by a clever-stone.

"I bin go along Cherbourg in Queensland one time," he said. "Them wild blackfellows there give me a stone. They said this stone would make me lucky at gambling. I don't do no gambling, but as the power in that stone built up, it made me take to drink.

"One night I got to drinkin' hard, and I was so sick I made up my mind to chuck that there stone away.

"I threw that stone away. Then I heard 'whizz, thump' and that stone landed back at my feet, bein' a real clever-stone. I threw it away again and 'whizz, thump' it came back again.

"By golly, I said, I got to get rid of this stone, and I chucked it as far as I could and started to run. That stone come back whizz through the air and hit me on the head and made me silly so I had to go to hospital.

"I dunno where that stone is now, so I reckon I got rid of it all right. Pretty likely I'll get well now."

Having established that hypnotism occurs in aboriginal society and that it is, indeed, an integral part of their magic, it was desirable to find out if hypnotic procedures effective with white people were equally as effective, or perhaps more so, with them.

One of the features that would differ from aboriginal practices, of course, would be that the operator would not have the prestige of the clever-man and would not be clothed in a magical atmosphere. His own prestige as a white man would be quite considerable, but somewhat different.

The aboriginal clever-man continues to maintain prestige among his people, even when the tribe has broken up, largely because of his ability as a hypnotist. He maintains an atmosphere of credulity about himself. And he will descend to sly opportunism or even outright deceit to keep this atmosphere or enhance it. Even thoroughly sophisticated natives will affirm that doctors can perform any variety of amazing feats. If a doctor declines to do anything such as cure a person or disperse a storm, it is not because he is unable, but because he does not want to do it. It is rather more than a royal prerogative; he has a sort of godlike quality. Because of this his prestige impact is very considerable.

Although I had hypnotized white subjects with some success, I was anxious that this experiment should be in very capable hands. I was assisted by Laurie Enticknap, an experienced operator.

His two subjects were Owen Anderson and Lance Walker, whom we visited at Churchill, about thirty miles from Brisbane. To get away from the women on this serious business, we drove to Goodna and found a pleasant, shady spot on the banks of the river.

The results he obtained in a rather brief session Laurie considered showed that Owen and Lance were at least as readily hypnotizable as any two relatively naïve white subjects chosen at random.

Lance Walker, a young full blood in his early twenties, was the first subject. Suggestions were given first of all in the waking state. He was induced to raise his hand from where it was resting on his knee when it was suggested that it was feeling lighter. Anesthesia of the arm was produced, and Laurie pulled numbers of hairs from his arm with no indication of pain being felt.

"Hey, Lance," cried Owen, incredulously, "you don't feel that?" Putting out his own arm he said to Laurie, "You do it to me so it don't hurt."

Laurie suggested that Owen's arm would become insensitive to pain. That the native yielded to his gentle persuasion was evident when the hairs were pulled from Owen's arm and his eyes opened wide with wonder.

"Well, what do you know!" he cried. "That didn't hurt a little bit. I reckon that's real clever."

Laurie returned his attention to Lance Walker. In something less than five minutes he had produced a hypnotic trance. While Lance was in the trance state, simple tests were carried out, a posthypnotic suggestion given that was subsequently heeded, and simple hallucinations were induced. Following these, amnesia was suggested.

"When I wake you up, you won't remember anything that's happened," said Laurie.

When he woke Lance, the other native was anxious to see if this incredible thing could have happened. "Do you remembers what happened to you?" asked Owen.

"Remembers what?" asked Lance, dreamily.

"Remembers what Mr. Enticknap said—how you was walking down the street and you seen a funny fellow and you laughed out loud—don't you remembers that?"

"How could I remembers anything?" said Lance. "I bin havin' a good sleep."

"What do you know!" said Owen.

"You can remember now," said Laurie, quietly—and Lance could!

A hypnotic trance state was again induced.

"You like music," said Laurie.

"That's right," replied the entranced Lance.

"You can play the guitar pretty well."

"That's right."

Picking up a stick lying near by, Laurie placed it in Lance's hands, saying, "Here's your guitar. Tune it up."

Lance tuned his imaginary guitar.

"Now let's hear you sing your favorite song, Lance. What is it?"

" 'Bimbo,' " replied Lance and, clearing his throat, burst forth melodiously.

Anyone passing by would have been amazed to see our group on the river bank: Laurie calmly watching his subject's reactions, myself jotting hurried notes on a pad, Owen, open mouthed and incredulous, and Lance, his eyes closed, swaying gently as he strummed at the stick and sang the popular song, "Bimbo."

They would not have realized that a considerable step forward in explaining aboriginal magic was being taken.

CHAPTER 13

Women in Magic

At first glance it would seem that aboriginal women live merely on the fringe of magic. Ignoring the minor part that women play in some magico-religious ceremonies, including portions of the initiation rites, a little love magic, and a few unimportant minor rituals, magic appears to be essentially a male activity in aboriginal society.

This, however, is not the case. Men tend to dominate magic, it is true, but the role of women is far from insignificant. They play their part, for example, in magical increase ceremonies; on Fraser Island, off the Queensland coast, women used to sing magic songs and swing bull-roarers to ensure plentiful supplies of fish and honey. This function has much the same purpose as increase ceremonies in which men are dominant, where the prime idea is to secure the fecundity and plentifulness of particular groups of animals or plants corresponding to the groups conducting the *corroborees*.

Among the Aranda a woman very occasionally used to act as a sort of female *kurdaitcha*. The sorcery was always carried out at her husband's behest and never after consultation with tribal elders. To prepare his wife, the man would grease her with fat and red ocher and, using blood drawn from himself, decorate her with cockatoo down. In one hand she would carry a decorated club, and in the other a stick charmed by her husband. With this stick it was believed she would magically injure her victim. It was thrown toward him and believed magically to enter him and make him sick.

An interesting secondary feature associated with this sorcery was a superstition that the failure of the female *kurdaitcha* to achieve her object would be shown by the behavior of a small tuft of rattails retained by the husband. He attached these to a digging stick thrust in the ground, and while his wife was absent on her nefarious business, would watch them carefully. If they fell to the ground, he would believe that she had been discovered and killed, and immediately shift camp.

Women are occasionally recognized as doctors. The Dieri, a desert tribe living to the south of the Pitjendadjara, have even initiated women doctors. Usually these women are the widows of clever-men. They have acquired much of the husband's stock in trade of tricks, special songs, and magical passes, but usually confine themselves to the curing of simple ailments, telling the future, and providing love potions and charms. They never have a doctor's full powers, and in general it is thought that they cannot kill their victims by magic, but they can make them ill. They are believed to have special powers to harm the sexual organs of people magically, causing pain, impotence, and disease.

Women who establish themselves on the outskirts of the magical profession have not been associated with, and gained part of the power of, the great spirit world which is the source of the male doctors' magical strength; but occasionally these women claim such powers as the ability to make rain.

In her book, *The Euahlayi Tribe*, Mrs. K. L. Parker describes such a clever-woman. "Armed with this [clever] stick, a piece of quartz, some green twigs, and sometimes a stick with a bunch of feathers on top, and a large flat stone, she goes out to make rain. The crystal and stone she puts under the water in the creek, the feathered stick she erects on the edge of the water, then goes in and splashes about with the green twigs, singing all the time.

"After a while she gets out and parades the bank with the *wi-mouyan*, singing a song which charms some of the water out of the creek into the clouds, whence it falls where she directs it. Once my garden of roses looked very wilted. I asked Bootha to make rain, but just then she was offended with Matah [another native]. One of her dogs had been poisoned, she would make no rain in his country. However, at last she said she would make some for me. I bound her down to a certain day. The day came; a heavy storm fell just over my garden, filling the ground tank which was almost empty. About two inches fell. Within half a mile on each side of the garden the dust was barely laid."

The magical element in pregnancy is very considerable. Among the Aranda, Tjalkalieri had told me earlier, a couple who wished to have a child would visit a ratappa stone (there are numbers of them about the countryside), and carry out a short ritual there.

At the birth of children, old women, particularly the ones believed to be clever, exercise magical powers, especially if the birth be a difficult one. They chant potent songs, tempting the child to leave its mother's body. If this method happens to be unsuccessful, they wave a charmed stick over the expectant mother, threatening the tardy infant with punishment.

Old Susan Walker was fishing from the river bank at Tabulam when we mentioned this subject to her. It was a hot day, but Susan was wearing a heavy woolen pullover. Her only dress, hung on a bush to dry after washing, had had its top consumed by cattle grazing near her camp!

"Women doctors?" she said. "Yes, there bin women doctors long times ago. I recollects one time there was an old woman said she was clever. She used to help women who had babies coming——Wait a minute. I got a bite! No, missed him."

She hauled the line in, rebaited it, and skillfully cast it.

183

"One time there was a girl havin' a baby, an' she got in awful pains. She was rollin' about and moanin' fit to die. That baby was comin' the wrong way, peoples said.

"Them peoples didn't know what to do. Then one of them said, 'We better get that old clever-woman.' Well, this old clever-woman come along, an' she started talkin' to that baby, telling it to get the right ways round."

Susan hauled her line in again.

"Them tortoises keep pinchin' my bait," she grinned. "This old woman, I was sayin', talked away to this baby and in little whiles the woman what was havin' it got quieter and quieter. That old woman said, 'That baby's gonna be all right. I bin tellin' it.' And, sure enough, that baby was borned and it was a lovely baby. Now, I reckon that that old lady was clever, just like they nearly all was in the old time.

"You know, that same old woman used to take young babies and rub them and hold them up by the heels. She said this was to make them tall an' strong, and there wasn't none she touched that didn't grow to be a fine young fellow or girl.

"That woman used to say she bin through the rule."

By this Susan meant the woman claimed she had been initiated. In some tribes, indeed, initiation of girls did take place, though this initiation was not comparable in its extent with that experienced by young men.

Tooth evulsion sometimes was carried out. In addition the girls underwent a minor sexual operation, comparable with circumcision. This was a recognition of their approaching womanhood, since it was carried out at the appearance of the menses, and indicated their imminent role in the sexual and social organization of the group.

This has considerable implications for the aboriginal girl, for she now may become a participant in a magically sanctioned period of sexual license, which occurs in many tribes from time to time. In the Ooldea region, on the barren Nullarbor Plains, this is known as the *wongi* institution.

At predetermined times, under the terms of this institution, premarital and extramarital relations take place on a very liberal basis. These are periods when the normal restraints are withdrawn and all sorts of what otherwise would be irregular unions take place and are sanctioned.

Although we may condemn such practices as immoral, they do have a social justification in some tribes where old, influential, but possibly sexually inactive men have numbers of young, attractive wives. In these circumstances there are many young men for whom there are no women available. The *wongi* and similar institutions meet the needs of both these groups of younger people in particular.

On certain ceremonial occasions a ritual exchange of wives takes place. A particular example of this is when a revenge party is about to set out. Its members exchange wives as an expression of the deepness of their friendship.

When one party is about to attack another, the men may send over their wives as an offering if they wish to avoid a bloody encounter. If the wives are accepted (temporarily, of course) then no fight ensues.

This is often associated with what has been called the prostitution of native women. Whites coming into contact with completely tribal groups were surprised to find that women would be offered in friendship or to obtain some completely trivial material possession.

In aboriginal society, moreover, it was common earlier to find a system of secondary wives in operation. Thus a man might have one or more primary wives and a number of secondary wives, the latter being virtually lovers. They were referred to as "fancy girls" and women in such relationships (for a woman could be the primary wife of one man and the secondary of another) called their lovers "fancy men."

For their part women hold their love-magic *corroborees*, often in association with, but more often independent of, these institutions. These tend, of course, to promote further irregular relationships, as well as serving their primary purpose which is supposed to be the strengthening of marital ties.

Dr. Phyllis Kaberry, who witnessed a number of these *corroborees*, described one as follows: "The spectacle was a dramatic and vivid one. It took place in the vivid sunshine, against a background of red sandstone, the long yellow grasses and the barchinea trees with their crimson seed pods. The women themselves were greased with fat till their skins glistened; bold designs in charcoal, red ochre, and clay were drawn on their bodies, so that they seemed the living incarnation of the landscape itself; almost as though they had been impregnated with its harsh and vital colouring."

To some extent women control the temperament and perhaps the basic harmony of aboriginal society. When they sense the need for the excitement that follows their love magic *corroborees*, they organize them. This contributes to tribal solidarity. On occasions when tempers are on edge or feelings run high, they will go off into the bush in groups and carry out peace-making magic, or magic to prevent jealousy.

Some women doctors carry out cures in much the same way as do their male counterparts, but more often, in the tribe, women gather together and carry out what might be called group therapy, particularly if the patient be a woman. They will rub the patient with kangaroo fat and the life-giving red ocher, chant their songs that are supposed to purify and aid her and which must, at any rate, raise her spirits.

Their psychical experiences differ only slightly from those of men. They see visions, hear spirit voices, experience strange feelings; the essential difference is that the experiences of men are integrated into a system of esoteric lore—the Dream Time legends and the mythology of magic—so that, for example, the totem has a prime place as an explanatory device. Women have no part in the most profound ritualistic aspects of the aborigines' secret life; the role they play in the magic is unobtrusive but significant.

CHAPTER 14

Culture Clash

Selly was killed by *kurdaitcha*. Lyn and I knew him in Areyonga Valley. He was a young Pitjendadjara native who had tended rapidly to acquire western ways—he had had his hair cut the white man's way, for example, to the disgust of Tjalkalieri, Winjin, and other men. But Selly was not content. He wanted to remain part of the tribe as well—to partake of the lore, and to scoff at it, too. He was caught between two ways of life.

Often, as I talked with the old Pitjendadjara men about their secret life, Selly would sidle up to the group. The conversation invariably lapsed till, sensing that he was not wanted, the youth moved out of hearing again.

I detected an undercurrent of suspicion and the beginning of hatred, although at the time these things did not have full significance for me.

Lyn and I did not cultivate Selly. He was a nondescript native. But we noticed his preoccupation with the young girls of the tribe. With them he frolicked in the cool springs of the valley.

With them, too, he discussed some of the men's secrets. This is what the patrol officers were told when they came to investigate the "murder."

Selly was found with his neck broken. This is typical of

the actual violence that occurs in *kurdaitcha* killings, for these are political in nature. The magic is injected later—to bewilder and impress ordinary members of the tribe.

Selly was a victim of culture clash. In Central Australia the white man had shown himself to be superior in so many ways. He had many things to make his life comfortable. The white man could live without magic, could scoff at the blackfellows' superstitions. Selly could scoff at them, too, in the white man's way and, reveling in this new sort of freedom, talk openly to the girls about the secrets of the men of the tribe. But not with impunity. The tribal penalty, which he must have known, was death.

Selly's death had all the elements of tragedy: its inevitableness, its symbolism of the clash between cultures.

The Pitjendadjara are few in number but a proud people. The full impact of western ways they have not yet felt; a few missionaries, patrol officers, stockmen, and miners have been their only contacts; one or two natives, like Selly, have visited Alice Springs. They have moved out of their original tribal territory in the Petermann Ranges into that of the Aranda, but as a tribe they are still essentially intact. They have seen, and spurn, the breakdown of the Aranda. Unaggressive and unresentful toward whites, they still try to maintain their tribal solidarity. To do this, tribal law is zealously followed.

What probably happened in the case of Selly (and other natives who have died in the same way) was that his misdemeanors were carefully watched by tribal elders until they became so blatant that a council was called; it was then decided that, in accordance with tribal custom and tradition, he should die. A small party, probably only three or four, was chosen to carry out the *kurdaitcha* killing.

Besides the method of killing and the feather shoes said to be worn by the killers, the name *kurdaitcha* refers also to mythological creatures which, in the dualistic outlook of the natives, are spiritually responsible for the retribution that took place. It was a harsh warning to other youths who might have been considering following Selly's ways.

But the Pitjendadjara are now living under the white man's law, though they see little enough of it, and cases of murder—for that is what the white man calls these killings—are dealt with in our courts of law. Be it said, though, that the beliefs and motives of the natives are in some measure considered in these cases.

Three natives were arrested by patrol officers and tried for murder at Alice Springs. They admitted the killing and were moved to a jail far away from their tribal area.

The conflict between the two cultures is temporarily resolved with the trial and conviction of the natives actually responsible—the tribe has removed the unit that threatened it, the white man's law has exacted its penalty.

But the problem continues; the conflict goes on. Every now and again a news item reflecting the problem finds its way into a city paper. One recent account reads in part: "Twenty aborigines from two tribes fought fiercely with spears, boomerangs, and nulla nullas for half an hour on Saturday night. The battle began after a lubra had claimed that the elders of a Roper River tribe had 'sung' her 17-year-old son to death."

It is merely a sample of the sort of conflict that takes place in aboriginal society, and in which we must now inevitably interfere.

Aboriginal society is rigidly disciplined. Its laws may not always be sound according to our views. But when we move into aboriginal territory and deliberately, as in the case of missionaries, or incidentally, as in the case of large cattle stations, break down the tribal organization and way of life, without substituting something tangible and understandable in their place, confusion, misunderstandings, and tragedy inevitably follow.

Merely moving herds of cattle into aboriginal country can create untold trouble. The cattle eat the natural herbage, trample and destroy the roots, and frighten away the game, so that hunting within twenty miles or so of a mission or station may become impossible. A native who spears cattle, even though he be hungry, is severely dealt with.

The white man solves this problem by employing the natives or making them gifts of white flour, tea, and sugar, and thus creates a further problem.

When aborigines are employed on cattle stations—and they are magnificent stockmen—they are paid a mere pittance, about a twentieth of what a white man would be paid, and given a few rations. Economically, however, they are indispensable to the white station owner. He could not run his station without them. For this reason some of the camp hangers-on, who do not work, are also given rations.

The aboriginal, accustomed to spending long hours learning bushcraft as a youth, and being occupied with hunting as a man, now comes by a less satisfactory diet, often without much effort. He soon loses the ability to live off the land, as the Aranda have done, loses his virility, and with idle time on his hands falls into arguments, mostly about women. The women themselves have much more free time now that they don't have to dig yams, root out witchetty grubs, or perform the other womanly chores of the tribal life.

It is not only in the tribal and near-tribal areas that the conflict goes on; nor is it only in the case of killings, or "murders," that white interference creates misunderstandings and friction. The conflict ranges down to trivial things like unlicensed dogs—in these cases aboriginal resentment is often the more bitter.

Such was the pathetic case of old Fred Cowlin and his dogs. Fred, a harmless old man so far as the white community was concerned, and one doing a great deal of good among his own people and much respected by them, has as his tribal totem the dingo. All dogs therefore come under his protection; and at one time he had nearly a hundred living with him; we saw him once with nearly fifty, on another occasion with about thirty. The dogs fared for themselves; they hunted wallabies and rabbits. They lived about Fred's camp, shared his bark shelter with him and his wife Bella.

However, in the white man's law, it is an offense for a person to own an unlicensed dog. Such dogs may be destroyed by a police officer. For this noble work the policeman receives a bonus of two shillings, six pence (about twenty-five cents) per head.

Consequently, when Fred's pack grew to any size, it was customary for the police officer in the township near where Fred was camped to destroy the animals and thus earn a few pounds.

Discussing this pointless slaughter with us, natives emphasized, "That police fellow didn't *have* to do it. Them dogs and Fred never did no one no harm. And they was Fred's *djurabeels*, too."

We are fortunate that the aborigines have always been few in number and quite unaggressive. There were a few cases in the early days when natives walked up to outback stations with their hands in the air as a sign of friendship, but dragging spears in the grass with their prehensile toes, and massacred the whites for the sake of a few bags of flour; but these instances were not common, nor were they typical.

Aborigines did not retaliate when the early white settlers shot them for sport, and they do not retaliate now when the whites instead direct their viciousness to their dogs.

There are two separate social problems with the aborigines today. One is concerned with people who still are intact as tribes, who still hunt, fish, and dig roots, who still initiate their youths, and who are bound by magical tradition and lore.

These are people who have adapted themselves very successfully to a harsh physical environment. They eke out an existence in desert areas where white men would perish. They have not become agricultural people because there are no grains indigenous to Australia; but in some areas they harvest tiny grass seeds and make a kind of flour from them. And the native Australian has no beast of burden. With the exception of the extreme north where there are crocodiles, there has been no menace from fierce animals.

The aborigines have retired into themselves and with their introspection and contemplation have developed what is to them a highly satisfactory spiritual culture. Initial culture contact does little damage to this.

They are extraordinarily responsive to external influences and often in a surprising way. Professor Elkin a few years ago contacted an Arnhem Land tribe whose association with whites he thought to have been nil. In observing one of their *corroborees* he was astonished to find the players going through actions that could only be imitations of shuffling, dealing, and playing cards. He found that during the war a few Australian troops on exercises had penetrated into this area.

Problems arising from culture contact are often small enough in themselves—cumulatively they have been, and are, disastrous.

The economic organization of aborigines, for instance, is very simple. With few material possessions there are few economic worries. Food is shared. What economic system exists is socialistic in nature.

With the introduction of money payments and desirable material possessions, numbers of difficulties have arisen. Unused to budgeting, aborigines have dissipated their earnings. Gambling is but one of the problems.

One of the Aranda artists in Central Australia, whose earnings in an exhibition had been quite considerable, had his funds administered by a committee of whites because of his foolish spending—fireworks, for example, which are immensely popular with the desert natives.

This native had, in a short space of time, bought two radios. He approached a member of the white committee for some of his money to be released to him to buy yet another set. In response to questioning, he said he wanted another set because a knob on his latest purchase was loose!

In their natural state aborigines are quite unused to the idea of saving—food is consumed as it is gathered or hunted—and they cannot grasp the idea that money is a medium by which value can be stored. The problem of education here is more difficult than would first appear: fundamental concepts have to be disturbed.

Diet is yet another worry. Their natural diet, though often meager, is well balanced. With the introduction of white flour, tea, and sugar, and the near disappearance of game from their diet, nutritional diseases have exacted a severe toll. Industrious natives make damper, which is a large scone made with flour and water, but I have seen natives mix a liquid, gluey mess with white flour, sugar and water, which they drank.

Hygiene? In the tribe when a bark shelter, or *wurlie*, becomes unhygienic, its occupants vacate it and build another. As natives cluster about cattle stations and missions, however, they follow the white man's pattern and adopt more permanent dwellings, often made of corrugated iron and bags. In time these become unhygienic because the natives are not used to caring for permanent dwellings, and diseases follow.

With their often enforced idleness, morals as well as morale deteriorate. Natives present a picture of misery and degradation, a picture that is humiliating both to themselves and to us.

As the breakdown of the tribe advances, delinquency and crime develop. The numbers of half-castes increase, the tribal law (often strict as we noticed in the case of Selly) peters out, and the worst of white vices are embraced. Mostly, it would seem, this is for want of appropriate education in simple economics, health, and hygiene. But perhaps the problem is not so simple.

There are two main schools of thought. Oversimplified,

their ideas are, on the one hand, to educate and assimilate the aborigines in a planned, organized way and, on the other, to let them live in their natural state in inviolable reserves.

What of the other main group of aborigines? These people, now predominantly caste-natives to whom tribal life is often not even a memory, who live in groups on government stations or in shanty towns on the outskirts of country centers, are bound together by social attitude toward them, by their still magically rich culture, and in a few cases by clever-men.

They are sensitive to white opinion of them; but they have no spirit. They are indolent and unreliable as workers. They have accepted the harsh social environment thrust upon them by the white community with the same equanimity as their brothers in the desert accept their harsh physical environment. But they are not adapting themselves as well to it.

Their passivity would seem to be a racial trait. Be that as it may, the problems of housing, hygiene, sanitation, diet, economics, morals, and morale appear to be magnified—a hundredfold in their case—and the situation is the more pitiable because they seem unable or unwilling to make the effort to improve themselves. They are too ready to accept their lot.

We have a vicious circle of white prejudices and discrimination hindering the social improvement of the aborigines. The natives have accepted that they are of inferior status, and the attitude of whites is tending to perpetuate that view. They have had most of the responsibilities of our culture thrust on them, but with few of the privileges. They cannot vote, for example.

Assimilation into the white community does not necessarily mean interbreeding. This has occurred, of course, and has unfortunately been the main medium of the racial breakdown. It has been unfortunate because aboriginal girls have associated, for the most part, with the worst type of whites. Most of the relationships have been transient, very few on even a semipermanent basis.

This introduction to white culture has not been edifying for the girls. For their children it is even worse. They are often neglected, wanted by neither parent, and are either brought up by older relatives or become state wards.

A few years ago a young and attractive quarter-caste aboriginal girl at Coff's Harbor, one who had obviously thought about her problem, said to me, "A white man has asked me to marry him. He's got a good job. He wouldn't live with my people, of course, and I'd be shamed to live like white peoples. Later on my children would be shamed to go to the white school."

Unscrupulous whites have used liquor to seduce aboriginal girls. Wine has been supplied to natives in return for labor. A short time ago in northern New South Wales a field of corn would be picked by a native in return for one bottle of cheap wine worth less than fifty cents.

Supplying intoxicating liquor to aborigines naturally has become a serious offense. Even the supply of methylated spirit (denatured alcohol) for lighting stoves on government settlements is watched very closely, for natives have been found to make the most surprising concoctions.

This problem, however, has its amusing side. At Woodenbong, in the early days of our investigations there, Bertie Mercy became violently drunk. He told us later that this was the result of his discussing magical lore with us. His children and grandchildren had mocked him, calling him a "superstitious old blackfellow," and he had had a few drinks.

When other residents complained about Bertie's behavior, the manager visited his hut to search for the liquor. There he found a bottle of evil-looking, foul-smelling liquid which, believing it to be one of their strange intoxicating concoctions, he confiscated.

A few days later, Bertie, now sober, made a number of boomerangs. These he was accustomed to decorate and sell to occasional tourists in nearby townships. When he came to finish them off he found that his bottle of varnish had disappeared!

Natives on the settlement missed the humor of the situation. They confided to us, "The manager is terrible. He stole Bertie's boomerang mixture."

Gambling, too, is a problem, for aborigines are not used to moderation. At settlements like Woodenbong and Tabulam a few natives have regular jobs at nearby farms, dairies, and sawmills. Their money comes into the camp, and at gambling rings is redistributed. No one seems to mind, least of all those who do no work but who sometimes win a little. Girls are given "a start" at the gambling schools and for the loan of this money repay with favors.

For aborigines, money comes and goes quickly; they are careless and carefree about it. It is not unusual to find a native spending an entire week's wages to hire a taxi to a football match a couple of hundred miles away. More often than not he does not even have the return fare.

Most of the elderly natives are keenly sensitive to the delinquency and crime into which their offspring slip so readily. Bertie Mercy said, "My children are criminals." Another declared, "My children are not black or white. In the old days when there was law [i.e., aboriginal law] they would have been killed by the old fellows."

Strangely, the problem of the aborigines has not been tackled on a national basis in Australia. Each state controls aborigines in its territory. Most are acutely aware of the difficulties of assimiliation. For example, in a circular the Aborigines Welfare Board of New South Wales stated, "Unfortunately, aboriginal communities . . . have not been inspired to emulate the customs of the white community because that community has not conceded a place in their social ranks for aborigines. It is not surprising in these circumstances that aborigines are disposed to seek such relaxation as may be available to them, and it is inevitable as a result that there should be a deterioration in moral standards, excessive drinking and a disposition towards any kind of activity that will afford relief from a dead-end existence."

This board sees the problem as one of education, so that aborigines may gain "an adequate appreciation of the benefits to be derived from better housing, hygiene, health and education [and] a recognition of the obligations they owe to their families and to the community in which they hold citizenship."

But, besides the social limitations that have been set on them, aborigines have drifted into a limited labor market, mostly because they have been deprived of training that would suit them for anything other than the simplest and most menial occupations.

A paradox, however, has also arisen. For, although white authorities have done too little for aborigines in that they have failed to face up to such basic problems as suitable education, social instruction and supervision, they have also done too much. They have provided free housing, rations for all but able-bodied men, free medical and dental treatment, and so on; they have tended to produce a race of parasites who will not work when they can draw social service and unemployment benefits, or receive aid from relatives. However, some natives I have known had not sufficient wit, initiative, or energy even to claim government benefits to which they were entitled.

Although the clever-man still wields considerable influence in these disintegrated societies, that influence is now limited in a number of directions. He may, however, be a key to the solving, in part at least, of some of the social problems of his people.

Education is fundamental and important to the rehabilitation, both social and economic, of the aborigines. It alone, however, cannot be sufficient. With it must come a rebirth of the proud tribal spirit, a resurgence of their language and culture, a reorientation of their racial consciousness. This can best come from, or be guided by, aboriginal clever-men, the priests of their way of life and, in detribalized groups, they are, unfortunately, now so few.

The greatest difficulty, however, lies in the fact that, no matter how sympathetic our views about them may be, it is becoming increasingly evident that fundamentally they are different from us.

CHAPTER 15

Savage or Sage?

Groups of people differ very considerably from each other. We are all human beings, yet each one of us is individual and differs from his fellows in some ways; and the various groups—races, societies, or cultures—differ from each other in greater or lesser degree in a wide variety of characteristics.

The differences are most clearly seen in physical qualities. No one would mistake an African pygmy for a Chinese or an Eskimo or a Red Indian. Almost any single characteristic— skin pigmentation, hair structure, skeletal form—would be sufficient to identify the pygmy; the collection of the multitude of racial characteristics in the individual makes the evidence for difference overwhelming. Similarly, there are mental differences.

The differences between individuals within the one culture provide the raw material for the multitude of intelligence and aptitude tests now so common. Some individuals have a facility for abstract reasoning, others excel in linguistic or mathematical ability, or have an extraordinarily retentive memory. Between racial groups there would also seem to be differences. Some of these may be innate, but most appear to be acquired and developed according to racial needs, standards, and cultural trends. For example, native peoples lacking a written language, as the Maoris of New Zealand, are often able to recite genealogies extending over scores of generations. Mental differences are rather subtler and harder to differentiate than physical differences.

In recent years, there has been a tendency to minimize the differences between peoples in the, I believe, mistaken hope that this will lead to a wider understanding between them. We cannot, however, ignore the differences, and it is only by recognizing, examining, and trying to understand them that the points in common can be seen in their true light.

There are many reasons why groups of people differ from other groups. In the case of the aborigines, for example, one important reason is that there has been a long period of isolation from other peoples. The latest estimates place this at ten thousand years, at least.

The aborigines of Tasmania, now extinct, were Negroid; the mainland natives do not fit well into any major ethnic group, and have been called Australoids. There is some evidence of their having originated from Dravidians, people from India.

Culturally the aborigines belong to the Stone Age. Their material culture is of the most primitive sort. They have no knowledge of metal, working of pottery, or agriculture. Their implements are neolithic in character.

What are some of the mental characteristics of aborigines? Tribal natives are alert, as their harsh natural environment demands, but lacking intercourse with other peoples, having no written language and a wide range of comparatively unrelated dialects, they appear backward when viewed against the background that a white society has thrust into their cultural scene. To the average white observer detribalized natives appear lethargic and dull-witted.

The advent of white culture brings many problems of assimilation to native peoples. Some natives, such as those of New Guinea, particularly on the coast, have adjusted themselves readily to the new demands on them. The Australian aborigines, however, have found difficulties and unfortunately have not risen to these difficulties: groups of them living in government settlements or on the outskirts of country towns fall victim to indolence and despair; they appear to drift whither the currents of their environment take them and, on the surface, appear content to drift.

Formal education has so far been singularly unfruitful in assisting the assimilation of aborigines. The fault may indeed lie with the system of education itself rather than the natives. We know that, to date, they have failed to benefit academically and socially from it. Despite liberal assistance and encouragement, not one aboriginal has, to my knowledge, earned a university degree; only a handful have finished high-school; most evade school completely if they can. They lack personal incentive and ambition—why should they attempt to compete in an academic struggle against more favored whites when to succeed will only mean a separation, if not physical at least cultural, from the more or less integrated aboriginal group of which they are so much a part?

In general their social progress has been disappointing, but a few outstanding individuals, such as the tenor Harold Blair and the growing coterie of Aranda painters headed by Albert Namatjira, have earned honored places in our art world. Others, like Captain Reg. Saunders, having distinguished themselves in the armed services.

Because education is thought to be the key to correcting social and cultural shortcomings, the failure of most aborigines to benefit from it is disturbing. Lyn and I therefore welcomed the opportunity to carry out an investigation for the Australian Commonwealth Office of Education on the conditions influencing the educability of aborigines. We were interested, too, in primitive modes of thought which, we considered, give rise to and sustain magical beliefs and practices.

The Commonwealth Government is acutely concerned with

the relative failure of aborigines to benefit through education, despite the fact that aboriginal schools are staffed by qualified and sympathetic teachers, that consideration is given to the harsh environmental circumstances of aborigines, and that modifications are made in the standard curriculums within the different states. It has had some success in comparison, for example, with mission schools which are rarely able to take their pupils beyond third grade — approximately halfway through the primary school work. Government schools take quite a number of aboriginal children right through the primary grades, though very few actually qualify to continue their education in high school.

We carried out the investigation with the school children at Woodenbong. We were keenly aware of the influence of culture in most, if not all, of the recognized intelligence tests— a problem that has been confounding psychologists for many years—and decided to use selections from numbers of recognized tests, in conjunction with others that seemed to us to be particularly pertinent to the situation as we knew it. We planned a test battery that was as comprehensive as we could make it, for we wished to explore in some degree every phase of the aboriginal child's ability.

We were not interested in finding some absolute standard of intelligence, or sociality, or educational adjustment. The value of using portions of standardized tests was that we could compare the results of these Woodenbong children with the established standards of the white community towards which their assimilation is presumably directed. Our own additional subtests were aimed at sorting out what we thought were probably significant factors that might not otherwise be shown up. And there was a good deal of value to be derived from examining a number of subjects with the same measuring stick even though that had been derived, for the most part, from another culture.

Our test battery was based on that used by Judith Andrews, of Queensland University, in a comparison of the performance of home-domiciled children with orphanage children. Her study showed a significant difference between these groups favoring those living at home and having the benefit of a friendly, sympathetic, and helpful environment.

Mental testing with any subjects, under any conditions, is fraught with dangers—mainly of misinterpretation. We had learned only too well, as in the case of Tjalkalieri, that beneath a seemingly dull brown visage might lurk depths of wisdom and understanding that could easily go undiscovered. At Woodenbong we expected to find huge gaps in general knowledge, a lack of verbal ability, social inadequacy, and other deficiencies arising, for the most part, from a thoroughly wretched environment. The tests confirmed our worst fears. The poor performance of our aboriginal subjects reflected the inadequacy of mental tests derived from one culture applied to another (although these did show interesting differences in modes of thought) and the influence of a miserable environment and the attitude of hopelessness it engenders.

We tried to see the results of all the tests in their real setting—a settlement of a couple of hundred aborigines, relatively homogeneous, where there are close personal relations. The native dialect, mostly Bundulung, is widely spoken. Even tiny children are often bilingual—without real competence in either language.

In some cases the family housing is adequate; in a large number the accommodations are crowded, untidy, and dirty. Few, if any, of the school children have a bed in which they sleep alone. Usually beds are shared with other children and with adults. In some cases blankets and bags on the floor are the only bedding. Often, due to overcrowding, and also to be close to the only fire in the house, children sleep in the kitchen. Most of the children sleep in the clothes—sleazy, worn castoffs from whites—they wear during the day. Few of the homes have adequate lighting; often there is no light beyond that provided by the fire in the stove, or by a brazier. Some children sleep out of doors, even on the coldest nights.

The distressing plight of the young children was vividly illustrated for me one night when I sat with an aboriginal family around a brazier talking. At about nine o'clock Pattie, a schoolgirl of six, fell asleep as she crouched by the fire. She was placed, as she was, beneath some bags in the corner of the room.

Bathing and washing facilities are very limited. Only one or two homes have large tubs. In these circumstances it is difficult for a child to keep clean. Most of the children tested were obviously suffering from head-lice infestation.

Many of the children came to school in the morning without having had any breakfast and with little prospect of a midday meal. The Aborigines Welfare Board provided cocoa and bread and butter during the morning break, and we saw many of the children eating ravenously. Their diet is poor. Often aboriginal mothers will not go to the trouble of cooking a meal; when they do it is rarely more than a damper and a cup of tea, though sometimes a thin stew is made. Even mushrooms are eaten raw.

There are some better class homes, and at these the parents, usually caste-natives, are sometimes equipped, though not well, to provide that background of common knowledge so important to a school child. In most of the homes, however, the questions likely to arise in a curious child's mind must go unanswered.

The school child often lives in a home atmosphere that can only, by white standards, be described as vicious. In the stages where moral training by example is so important, it is not merely missing but is replaced by immorality. This is, of course, immorality by our standards. In a small three-room house it is not unusual to find all fourteen or fifteen occupants, including school-age children, sleeping in the same room—together with any visitors who happen to drop in!

In a white child's environment the home is a place where peace, comfort, instruction, and security are generally to be found. In the case of most of the children tested, the home environment creates more problems than it can solve.

Parents do not generally seek medical or dental treatment for their children or themselves, except in case of pressing emergency, although these are freely available to them. They are able to suppress discomfort and even pain in themselves by self-suggestion, a hang-over from the tribal days, but this is a treatment of the effect and not the cause. Their children do not appear to have the same ability, or stoicism, and thus suffer unnecessarily.

Apart from school activities, play is not organized. Books and newspapers are in general not bought or read. There are, as yet, no local activities such as Boy Scouts or Girl Guides to provide interests. Hobbies are unknown.

Such were the conditions we found—indications of the complex of social behavior, interests, beliefs, and attitudes, often of a primitive nature, that an aboriginal child "inherits." The environment was slumlike; school children lived in circumstances closely approximating those of poor whites, and it is with them that they are, in this respect, most comparable. But the means of correcting many of the adverse environmental conditions were often well within reach of the natives themselves, if they cared to make the necessary effort.

Some natives at Woodenbong were earning relatively high wages at local sawmills and farms but squandered their money in gambling, unnecessary taxi trips to distant football matches, and so on, while they lived in miserable, uncomfortable, and unpleasant shacks that could have been improved by linoleum, curtains, and simple inexpensive furnishings. Often their children lacked, in some degree, both food and clothing.

We had known these people at Woodenbong for a long time and our testing was thus facilitated. We knew something of their language, we knew their tribal and family background, and that, with certain reservations, they accepted us. Knowledge of the language was important, for we found tiny tots giving answers to some of the test questions in the native dialect, softly and timidly, and they could easily have been misunderstood.

The test battery we decided on was a most comprehensive one—we planned to plumb the depths.

In the main test there were twelve subtests. Some of these were drawn from standardized intelligence tests. The first, for example, came from the Wechsler Intelligence Scale for Children. It was simply a set of thirty general knowledge questions ranging from "How many ears have you?" to "What is a lien?"

Comprehension was tested with the next subtest. It included questions like "What ought you to do when you are hungry?" and tested fairly difficult behavior and attitude problems with questions like "Why should we judge a person more by his actions than his words?"

Ideas of similarity were called for in a subtest that asked, for example, "In what way are an apple and an orange alike?" Likenesses between ocean and river, egg and seed, asleep and awake were asked for. This subtest proved to be singularly useful, for it showed up weaknesses in concept formation and a mode of thinking characterized mainly by deficiencies in the inductive processes of thought. It showed weaknesses in vocabulary and the need for our subtest probing this ability.

In western culture verbal ability correlates fairly highly with intelligence, which is to be expected, since the highly intelligent person acquires a substantial vocabulary and is usually adept in word usage. A standardized vocabulary scale —from the Wechsler Intelligence Scale for children—was also used. While this scale was developed for white subjects, it provided a very wide range and was, we considered, adequate for any group expected to have reasonable facility in English— such as detribalized caste aborigines.

Numbers of items requiring activity by the children were included. Principal of these were the block design subtest in which the subject copies simple designs with colored blocks, and the Porteus maze test, already used by Professor Porteus among the Aranda and thought by him to be a good measure of intelligence free of cultural influences.

An entire subtest was devoted to time; in this the attempt was made to measure development of the concept of time relations. It included questions like "What are the names of the days of the week?" and "Is a month longer or shorter than a year?" The children were asked also to read the time from a clock and, among other things, to arrange half a dozen pictures of a man, from babyhood to old age, in the right order.

A similar inquiry into number names and concepts was made with questions like "How many fingers have you on your left hand?" and "If I divide an apple in half, how many pieces will I have?" The children were shown numbers of cards and asked, "Which card has a dozen dots on it?" and "Which has a score?"

Similarly we inquired into what we called orientation (the child's idea of himself and where he lives in relation to the rest of the world), and knowledge of money. Then we added a set of questions involving writing, identification of colors, identification of notable people, knowledge of the human body, and so on.

In addition, each child was given a complete Binet intelligence test (which, of course, is standardized on a white culture), and a picture-frustration test which was intended to probe for possible causes of mental disturbance.

How did the children face up to this ordeal of testing? They enjoyed it immensely. It was a welcome break from the boredom of formal lessons, for many of the tests were presented as games. The children's ages ranged from nearly six to fifteen. The average was about nine and a half.

The testing was fun for the children and provided many amusing moments for us. But before we had gone very far it was clear that a tragic picture, by white-culture standards, was emerging.

Conclusions we drew from analysis of the tests were far-reaching. They suggested basic problems that formal education cannot cope with—the lack of innate drive or personal incentives, the acceptance of standards of conduct vastly different from our own, and a passive resistance to formal schooling.

Our recommendations to the Commonwealth Office of Education, after the testing, referred of course to the children's harsh environmental conditions. More important in some respects, however, we thought, was the need for special training in inductive thinking in the form of what we called semantic games. A type of semantic game we suggested involved the children's sorting of, say, twenty common objects according to some principle—painted or unpainted, made from one material or several, graded according to value or usefulness, and so on—with another group of children attempting to discover the principle of classification.

We doubted very much, too, the efficacy of rote-learning and suggested a program of instruction rather more varied and interesting than the formal curriculum. The testing was carried out near the schoolrooms. In the background we could hear the teachers patiently, sympathetically, trying to teach the children the intricacies of, for example, compound interest (following the formal curriculum), while on our testing ground we found them floundering with basic numbers. Not one child in the school knew how many days there are in a year, for instance—but if compound interest is on the curriculum it must be taught.

But what were some of the interesting facts arising from the individual subtests? In the carefully graded general-knowledge questions, simple, concrete things were answered fairly well—but not one child of the thirty-odd tested knew who discovered America.

It might well be asked, "Why should they know who discovered America?" The point is that intelligence correlates quite highly with general knowledge and, while any one question might be challenged, a graded and standardized series enables, with certain reservations, one to be deduced from the other. And basic U. S. history is taught in Australian primary schools. Most white children early pick up such jingles as, "In 1492, Columbus sailed the ocean blue."

In the survey carried out by Judith Andrews this particular question was answered correctly by 75 per cent of the home-domiciled white children of about the same age as our subjects. In the same sized group of orphanage children 45 per cent answered correctly.

Practical questions in the comprehension set, such as "What ought you to do when you are cold?" elicited acceptable answers. However, the answer to the question "What is the thing to do when you are on your way to school and you are in danger of being late?" was almost invariably "Go home and wait till tomorrow"! This response, amusing to us, would have the full support of aboriginal parents, however.

In the tribal state aborigines have a glorious unconcern for time, which is very important in our culture. And in at least two families at Woodenbong the parents actively discouraged attendance at the settlement school. When we questioned them on this, they claimed that inferior teachers are appointed to aboriginal schools (rather the reverse is true), and they said this was proved by the poor results of aboriginal pupils. It was, of course, free to them to send their children to the ordinary school at Woodenbong Township, for there is positively no color bar, but the extra effort deterred them— that and possibly the knowledge that when aboriginal children had attended this and other mainly white schools, their performance had been equally disappointing.

Real trouble became apparent with the set of questions on similarities. More often than not differences were given and, although it was clear that there were intense verbal difficulties, it was also apparent that the concept of similarity was one that was just not grasped by even the oldest pupils.

One of the questions was, "In what way are wood and coal alike?" Despite the fact that coal seams occur in the immediate vicinity and, indeed, coal can be found in the creek about a hundred yards from the school, very few children knew what coal is or what it is used for. True, aborigines rarely, if ever, use coal (there is usually an abundance of firewood at settlements provided without charge by the Government) but with coal occurring nearby we expected its most common usage to be known.

Interestingly, the section intended as a test of vocabulary showed up clearly deficiencies in concept formation and knowledge of abstract things. While most children knew what a spade is, few knew what a nuisance is, and none knew what a fable is. This is, of course, in part a verbal deficiency and due to the lack of an aboriginal written language and the strong survival of "the lingo" at Woodenbong. There has been a resurgence of the aboriginal dialects in this area, which is perhaps an indication of a deep-rooted desire to return to the old way of life and reluctance to face up to the new.

The test with colored blocks in which they were asked to copy simple patterns found the youngsters hopelessly at sea. Twenty-two children failed to score at all on this test, despite rather more leniency in coaching and example than is allowed for in the standardized test. Not one child was able to complete the test; many of them were unable to comprehend what was required.

Why should a test like this prove so difficult? Construction toys are almost unknown among these and other aborigines. Unlike our children they don't amuse themselves with puzzles found in newspapers and magazines. The test was a clear example of the cultural influences that we incorporate, perhaps unknowingly, in intelligence tests intended for ourselves. It illustrated, too, how, almost unconsciously, we acquire a variety of skills and abilities through games and pastimes as children. Moreover, aboriginal children do not have the benefit of kindergartens or pre-school group activities—nor, for that matter, do white children in most rural areas. Although the prescribed or usual starting age for school is five, schooling is not compulsory until the age of seven, a fact of which many aborigines take advantage.

But, even bearing these things in mind, the performance of the aboriginal children was more than disappointing for the test did not require any unusual muscular co-ordination, or anything extraordinary in the way of special skills, and we expected far better results in a test with no verbal element in it.

In contrast the results on the Porteus maze test were most heartening.

Kinchika knew his way around hundreds of square miles of Australia's barren Center. As our camel team plodded along, he would gaze at the pattern of the ragged hills against the sky, readily identifying paths and foot tracks. Similarly, no doubt, he could interpret the strange maps of tribal country made by the elders on their *churinga* and marked on tribal dancing grounds. The detribalized natives also are conscious of their physical environment, the immediate countryside and natural features within a considerable radius.

It was then not surprising to find our aboriginal subjects performing well above average on the Porteus mazes. These tests consist of a series of graded mazes through which the subjects are required to indicate a path. Most of our child subjects at Woodenbong traced out, unprompted, with a finger the route to be taken and, given a pencil, moved quickly and accurately to completion of the task. In this test they displayed foresight, concentration, and application in a degree not shown in any other test.

The average chronological age of all the children tested was 9.6. The average mental age as shown by the maze test was 10.3 years—an apparent, but interesting, inflation of their real mental age.

One must wonder, of course, if this subtest was in fact relatively culture free and therefore gave a better interpretation of the aboriginal children's intelligence than any or all of the other subtests. This indeed may be so. Social anthropologists have found groups of natives who are socially efficient and adjusted to environment obtain a score so low as to seem absurd in tests standardized for European children.

In the remaining subtest the most striking feature was the weakness in relative concepts of all sorts. For example, the relative lengths of inches, feet, yards, and miles, the relative duration of months and years, were concepts grasped by very few children. There was, in general, a failure to be able to reason inductively, that is, to draw a general principle from a number of facts. Facility in this type of reasoning might well have a cultural basis in the case of whites and is usually found associated with social intercourse on the higher intellectual levels.

Number concepts and names caused untold difficulty, and similar trouble occurred with time. Very few children could tell the time (aborigines rarely have clocks, of course), and the concepts of "younger" and "older" were beyond most of them. Each child was asked, "Will you be older or younger when you are so old?" The age was always the child's own age plus four, so that a ten-year-old was asked, "Will you be older or younger when you are fourteen?" Only a handful of children answered correctly.

Although ideas of direction and local orientation were good, estimates of distance and length were extraordinary, considering that elementary measurements and measuring are, of course, taught at school.

"How tall do you think I am?" I asked an eight-year-old.

He looked at me solemnly for a moment or two and replied, "About two inches."

My ego was restored a little later when I asked the same question of a nine-year-old girl.

"Oh, you must be fifty feet," she said.

Poor scoring on some portions of the tests, despite liberal explanations, was undoubtedly due to failure to grasp the operative word or phrase in a question. The amplification of the question "What height am I?" by "How many feet am I?" was often misinterpreted as "How many feet have I?"

Vocabulary generally was both limited and poor in quality. In giving definitions, abstraction was at an extraordinarily low level. Definitions were given mostly by particular references. While a high level of abstraction is not envisaged as an educational target, the lack of this ability is a serious handicap to formal education and to adequate social adjustment.

Units of measurement caused a lot of trouble. One of the simple tasks set was to measure some short sticks. The children were handed a twelve-inch rule, and asked if they knew what it was and what it was used for. One lad went about his task seriously. He placed the rule at one end of the stick and carefully made a reading. Then he measured the length from the other end. Finally he placed the rule down and held the stick against it in a number of places.

"How long is it?" I prompted.

He hesitated for a moment and then replied, "Nine."

"Yes," I agreed. "Nine what?"

"Nine miles, I guess," he said.

Recognition of smaller denomination currency was good, although slang names were applied to all coins. Every child described a two-shilling piece as "two bob." Money calculations, however, in which the children actually held money to perform simple tasks such as change-giving, were very poorly done. Far more elementary teaching than compound interest was indicated!

In a group as large as the one we tested, the average I.Q., as measured by a standard intelligence test, should have been about 100. The average in the case of the aborigines, as measured by the Binet test, was 83.5 which is well down in the normal range and bordering on dullness. This would suggest that some of the results were very poor. This, indeed, was so. The lowest I.Q. recorded was 61. On the other hand the highest recorded was only 118.

While it may be unfair to use an intelligence test standardized on our culture as a measure for the aborigines, it is within our culture they are now attempting to live, because they cannot escape it, and by its standards they are judged. The general impression they give by white-culture standards is of dull-wittedness, and unfortunately this tended to be confirmed by the tests. The Binet test was not administered in an attempt to arrive at an absolute measure of intelligence, however. It was selected because it has two forms. It was envisaged that a retesting might later occur, when the second form could be used, and thus enable a comparison to be made. This situation did not eventuate.

The picture-frustration test consisted of a number of cartoonlike drawings depicting possible stress situations. One of the individuals is shown as saying something like this: "You are too little to play with us," or "You are a sissy," or "You are late for school." There is a space for the child shown in each picture to reply, and the subject tested is asked to say what he or she thinks the child would say.

The expectation is that the child will identify himself with the test character and to some extent reveal what his reaction would be in similar situations.

It would appear that this identification did take place, but the outstanding characteristic shown by this test was the lack of aggressiveness and, related to this, extreme submissiveness of the subjects. In response to the taunt, "You are a sissy," some boys replied in effect, "Yes, I know. I'm sorry."

Aborigines are submissive to whites, but not because they have been so taught. They have never been aggressive in the way that the Red Indians of North America or the Maoris of New Zealand were.

From the tests it was obvious that there were real problems in communication among our dark subjects. They were unable to use language as an effective tool of communication. One of the reasons, perhaps, was the extensive use of "the lingo" at home; the lack of reading matter was another. But, even bearing these things in mind, the deficiency caused us to pause and consider the situation.

Semantics, the relatively new science devoted to the study of language, meaning, and communication, had shown how critical verbal ability is to human intercourse. A review of aboriginal dialects showed that they were almost all very deficient instruments of communication—which is understandable considering the large number of dialects and the absence of a written form.

Moreover, the dialects revealed the outstanding deficiency shown by the tests—the lack of facility in concept formation, the ability to generalize, to think inductively. For example, an aboriginal dialect might well have hundreds of words relating to trees, a particular name for each particular type of tree, but no one word embracing all trees. In other words no word for "tree"—only words for "yellow box tree," "blue gum tree," "wattle tree," and so on.

Linked with all this were indications of a mode of thinking very unlike our own. Technically it would be known as "autistic" or "dereistic" thinking. In ordinary language, unrealistic or magical thinking.

Herein lies, I think, a basic mental difference between us and the aborigines. We form our generalizations (from which at the highest level we derive principles and natural laws) from a large number of experiences and observations. Having derived our principle, we test it against subsequent experience. Aborigines tend to derive principles from single experiences and observations, which is the very essence of superstitious thought, and do not critically test their assumptions.

Aborigines have no difficulty in assuming a close self-world relationship—a tacit assumption that everything that happens in the world has its impact on them and that, correspondingly, everything they do influences the world, mostly in a magical way. Ideas of cause and effect are wide and fantastic. There are mysterious unseen forces in the world influencing the natives, and within themselves they have mysterious forces by which they can influence the world. Their outlook is such that they bow to a frequently imaginary Fate.

But that very outlook, that mode of thought, was precisely the sort of responsive thinking in which telepathy, if it existed, would be most likely to occur, we thought, and in its occurrence be more vivid and realistic than the transitory experiences of white people.

Here was ground in which superstition and magic would flourish; but here, too, were the conditions in which psychical experiences might well far transcend those we know.

If there are language difficulties and difficulties in logic or mode of thinking to the solution of a problem (such as of communication) then the problem might tend to be solved without language and without logic by direct mind-to-mind communication.

"There is much we do not know," Tjalkalieri had said.

It was certainly true that aborigines have not developed a mode of reasoned thought in any substantial way resembling ours.

But could it not also be true that aborigines have plumbed depths of the mind, rich in their peculiar rewards, that we have left relatively unexplored?

And might it not also be true that, while they find it difficult to adapt themselves to our way of thought, we might indeed find it impossible to achieve theirs?

CHAPTER 16

Experimental

One of the aims of a research worker in the social sciences, whether he be a sociologist, a psychologist, or a parapsychologist, is usually to convert human beliefs, behavior, attitudes, and so on, to some quantitative form—to express them in figures. Considerable advantages usually result from this. But any human trait thus sought is extremely elusive; some, perhaps, still beyond our reach.

Could all the subtle aspects of aboriginal magic be reduced to statistics? And, if they could, what more about them could we learn? The statistics might, at least, show whether certain phenomena such as telepathy existed.

Our questionnaire, already put to a group of natives, had provided a large amount of case material, and from it we were able to obtain some interesting figures; for example, about half of the natives interviewed claimed to have actually seen a ghost.

We didn't always follow the exact wording of the questions, for often explanations and examples were necessary. Most of the subjects answered questions fully and, we believe, in good faith.

On the question of the reliability of informants a great deal might be said. In general, aborigines who volunteered information appeared to be less reliable than those from whom it was extracted with some difficulty. One native who had been an informant to a previous investigator of aboriginal folklore came forward with a great deal of generalized, stereotyped information that he might have acquired from any book on the subject—he was literate. But he could give few particular instances to illustrate the generalizations.

To certain questions informants replied, "Yes, boss. Those doctor fellows is so clever they could cure theirselves of their own death, if they wanted to," and "Yes, old Fred's clever all right. They say he was riding in the clouds on his cord one day and God Hisself gave him a Bible."

Such answers might tempt one to believe that there is no limit to aboriginal superstition—but our informants gave every evidence of being sincere. And, ignoring these few atypical answers, there remained a clear pattern of psychical experience and belief.

The first question asked was, "Would you know if a relative some distance away died, had an accident, or was seriously ill?" We followed this with a full probe on the belief of how this could occur, whether the subject had personally experienced such a thing, and so on. Only three of our subjects answered this question in the negative. Belief in this sort of supernormal ability was strong.

Unusual dreams were discussed, as was the place of the totem in mediating information; we probed for evidence of poltergeist phenomena associated with the doctors.

We asked about smoke signals, but in the Woodenbong area these were never common. Where information was to be sent over any distance, a runner carrying a message stick was used. The message stick guaranteed him safety when passing through enemy territory. Runners could travel up to seventy miles a day.

Every native interviewed was convinced that the aboriginal doctor has fantastic powers, that he could always know what was happening at a distance if such an event were relevant to the tribe, and that he could see into the future. Similarly, although little appears in the standard works suggesting that doctors might use hypnotism, every native said he had heard of doctors obtaining effects that were certainly hypnotic, and numbers gave firsthand accounts.

Most natives said they had heard of doctors making storms. One described them as "fellows of the wild winds."

Belief in the psychical powers of doctors and in the genuineness of ordinary natives' own occasional experiences was profound. But this very characteristic, which provides what may well be the perfect psychological background for the operation of psychical abilities at a high level of efficiency, is one of the things that hinders verification of some of the claims made—and makes laboratory-type testing desirable.

Aborigines are consummate storytellers. This is understandable. In the vastness of the Australian bush, the still, eerie nights of the desert, the facile raconteur is a man with an outstanding social asset.

The recital of myths and anecdotes plays a big part in their lives and it is likely they color and exaggerate accounts to enhance their storytelling value. This very characteristic, which might be suitable and proper in the lives of the natives, is a source of trouble for the anthropologist who wishes to record anything beyond the aborigines' stories as such. For the parapsychologist it is a positive danger. Yet it is not unlike some of the difficulties he faces in his own field when investigating such claims as telepathy among whites.

Most aboriginal accounts are impossible to verify within their own contexts. The anthropologist has to rely on consistency, cross-verification and, often, his own intuitive judgment. Parapsychology, dealing with phenomena like telepathy under the general title of "extrasensory perception," is compelled to discard anecdotal criteria (though the collection of anecdotes is usually a useful adjunct to the main investigation) and establish its own.

Aboriginal accounts can be compared with those reported by white people and within themselves can be cumulative and corroborative, but a statistical assessment was, we felt, very desirable, for science cannot waste its time with prolonged investigations or observations that would always be open to question.

In a large number of the narratives that Lyn and I collected there was prima facie evidence for the existence of telepathy, and it was to this problem we gave most of our attention. With a laboratory-type technique and statistical evaluation of the data obtained we could eliminate malobservation, hysteria, exaggeration, cunning opportunism, and deceit.

Such a technique, too, took adequate account of the vagaries of coincidence. There is a tendency in all societies for the unusual to take precedence over the usual, for successes to be remembered and failures forgotten. Thus a bias for the extraordinary develops. How much more pronounced is this likely to be in a society that places high value on psychical experiences!

Statistical methods also adequately met the objection that logical inference may possibly be responsible for some of the extraordinary accounts. An aboriginal clever-man is more likely to be right if he hazards that an aged, ill, or feeble person will die than if he pronounces the imminence of death overcoming a young, healthy tribal member; he may logically infer that it is a particular mob whose smoke is observed in a certain quarter if he knows the hunting habits of the groups; he can predict rain and "make" a storm if he observes subtle signs of nature that indicate rain. But he is not so favored when it comes to nominating the order of cards in a randomly shuffled deck he cannot see.

The techniques for the testing of extrasensory perception (or E.S.P. as it is better known) were evolved over many years. The most common method, with many variants, of course, was developed by Professor J. B. Rhine of Duke University, North Carolina.

It was Rhine's basic method that Lyn and I decided on for use with the aborigines. We used cards supplied by Duke University.

The deck was of twenty-five cards, five each bearing one of five symbols—cross, circle, star, square, and waves. Basically, the main idea is that, assuming a subject to be adequately isolated from any possible knowledge of the cards (that is, he cannot see them at all, or observe anyone who can, or hear unconscious whispering by anyone who can, and so on) he should, if he guessed the order of the symbols in a randomly shuffled deck, obtain no more successful guesses than would occur by chance. In the case of our deck this is five or thereabouts for each time through the twenty-five cards.

In a long series of guesses (many thousands are not unusual) any deviation from the expected average of five, which is described as the "mean chance expectation," can be statistically assessed and the odds against the result being a chance occurrence calculated.

The guessing of the symbols on cards may seem a far cry from some of the accounts of aboriginal telepathy we had recorded. But the difference is more apparent than real—the simple test covered the basic fact, took care of all the instances in which aborigines reveal knowledge of an event about which they could have no normal information and which they could not logically infer.

It was certainly an exploratory technique. It sought to establish, by methods that rule out the possibility of deception, exaggeration, and chance coincidence, whether or not aboriginal subjects could have statistically significant knowledge of events acquired by some means outside the usually recognized sensory channels.

The main objection to the test was that it had to take place under rigidly controlled conditions and took consider-

able time—widely different from the conditions under which
E.S.P., if it did occur, normally took place. We found that the
subtle influence of the experimenter, or the relationship between the subject and the experimenter, was critical.

We could not re-create the spontaneity of a life situation
with our test. We could, at best, take advantage of the natural
beliefs of our dark subjects and engender what interest and
enthusiasm we could with profuse encouragement and stimu-
lation.

In some cases, it seemed, psychical abilities were entirely
inhibited; in others the trigger was sprung for the release of
psychical energies, and outstanding results were recorded.

Lizzie Williams, known through the settlement as "Granny,"
was one of our first subjects. She was over seventy, a diabetic
and a cripple. But she was always cheerful, and a well-loved
disciple of the old-time.

Early in the mornings of the winter days when we began
our work at Woodenbong, we could rely on seeing her come
from her little cottage to where we were testing, wielding her
crutches vigorously, her bare feet barely skimming the frosty
ground.

She was one of the few natives who said, in effect, in response to our questionnaire, "No, I don't believe I can know
anything telepathically"—but she was the one native who
produced clearcut, unequivocal evidence of that ability.

Other natives obviously tried hard. We were the first white
people who had shown a sympathetic understanding of their
claims of mind-to-mind communication, and they were anxious
to demonstrate this ability if they could. But Granny was always relaxed and carefree. Perhaps this was the secret of her
success. Usually she made her guesses with a somewhat unruly
great-grandson on her knee, and interspersed her work with
observations and jokes.

The square she called "box," the circle, "*bool*," which is

the name for the initiation ring in her dialect, and so on. A typical piece of calling went something like this: "Box, *bool, kwiungun*—that's what we call star in the lingo—*bool* again, I think. Billie, you be good boy for your granny! *Kwiungun* ——You Sydney girl, missus? One time I bin go along Sydney. B-I-G place. Box, box, waves—you know what we call that fellow in the lingo——" And so it went on.

The remarkable thing was that this old woman was far exceeding chance expectation in most of her runs through the deck and building up an impressive total that, in terms of probability, represented millions to one against chance being responsible.

Naturally, we were very careful to ensure that there was no means by which Lizzie, or any other subject, could gain any ordinary knowledge of the cards.

During the tests the subject was not able to see the cards. This was ensured by having the subject, who guessed the cards, and the agent, who looked at them and attempted to send, separated by at least one wall. Usually I acted as the agent. The two people involved in the experiment were either in different rooms in the same building or, more often, one inside and one outside.

Lyn, who recorded the guesses, supervised the subject, and I watched the sending end. There were usually some onlookers—some natives seemed to do better in a spirit of friendly competition—but these were never allowed to be in a position to see and signal the identity of the cards.

The natives showed a ready recognition of the need for strict control of the tests and adjusted themselves to what were sometimes rather irksome conditions with good humor. There was no attempt at cheating here—although later, in the desert, mission natives made stupidly obvious attempts. Once a native acting as sender called out in dialect to the receiver, and that run was immediately canceled.

The usual procedure was for me to shuffle the cards thoroughly and the subject then began making guesses. When the deck had been run through, I took it to Lyn and we recorded the true order against the guesses. Then the deck was reshuffled, out of the subject's sight, ready for the next lot of calls.

In the first series at Woodenbong Lizzie Williams made 1,700 guesses. If chance alone had operated, she should have obtained somewhere about 340 hits. In actual fact, however, she scored 488.

Now the odds against this occurring by chance are fantastically high. We were satisfied that our test conditions were foolproof—we had tested Lizzie with onlookers, and by herself, in our makeshift laboratory in the old school building and in her own little cottage; there was no way she could have ordinary knowledge of the cards.

Moreover, other natives, some of them certainly more astute, had been tested under precisely the same conditions and, although some of the results were decidedly better than chance, they scored far less than this feeble old lady.

Here was the first clear evidence, statistically evaluated, of telepathy (or at least E.S.P.) among the aborigines.

Another interesting subject was Bertie Mercy. He did not make as many calls as Lizzie Williams, but his successes, like the over-all performance of the group, were also highly significant.

Naturally, Lyn and I were anxious to apply some of these tests to aboriginal doctors, and the opportunity came at Tabulam, for there we had as subjects Fred Cowlin and Edward Derry (Mumbi).

We stayed at the Tabulam hotel and daily walked the mile or so to the settlement. From the moment we left the hotel we were shadowed by aborigines, occasionally we caught glimpses of them flitting from bush to bush parallel with our track as we moved to the camp, and always there was the sentinel on the hilltop overlooking the approach to the camp.

Children would run screaming to their parents, *"Dalan,. dalan."* ("Whites.")

For some time there was an air of suspicion, but gradually it diminished and, with a discussion of various aspects of magic and sympathetic consideration of some of their personal problems, rapport was established and we were able to set up our test conditions.

Old Fred was a difficult subject. His desire to do well in the tests was overshadowed by his natural cupidity. His demands for tobacco and other small rewards were insatiable, and right from the outset he began to apply pressure on us. He would make his guesses seriously, often with good results, and then suddenly begin pattern-calling, running through the card symbols in precisely the same order over and over again. Whenever we called a halt to this play, he would look up with a sly grin and say, "More baccy, boss."

Eventually his demands became extortionate. After a particularly exasperating morning of pattern-calling, he walked over to a lap robe which Lyn had spread on the grass to sit on and asked for it!

With his deliberate attempts to obtain more than ordinary favors, Fred's attention obviously was not entirely on card guessing, and his records were vitiated by a mass of pattern-calling. Nevertheless his final score was above chance, although not significantly so.

Mumbi tried very hard and in his case, probably because of this very trying, a sort of reversal of effort took place and he scored below chance. At the time, too, he was most concerned about the health of one of his great-grandchildren.

But the two doctors were, all things considered, rather disappointing. No one had come anywhere near to the scores of old, crippled Granny.

Similarly, in Central Australia, the Pitjendadjara doctor, Winjin, although scoring above chance, did not reach the level of significance.

In this area, with test conditions rather different from those at Woodenbong, and difficulties of language in addition, we had two distinct groups of natives. First there were the Aranda, who had been under mission influence for several generations. They had lost much of their tribal organization and culture but, because of their isolation, had not become as sophisticated as the New South Wales people. The second group were the Pitjendadjara. Some had been in contact with whites for a matter of only a few years, in some cases months, and could be regarded as fully tribal.

These natives made, in all, 4,275 guesses and, once again, the chance expectation of 855 was exceeded, this time by 52. The interesting thing is that the tribal group scored very much better than the nontribal group. In 48 runs through the deck they contributed 41 of the excess of 52 hits. This score is statistically significant, and can be regarded as evidence of E.S.P. among tribal people.

But what if these results had been due to fantastic chance, that the million-to-one shot had come off? It was a possibility —we knew precisely how remote it was, thanks to the statistical techniques—but we wanted to satisfy ourselves.

After some years had elapsed since the first testing at Woodenbong, the opportunity occurred to work there again. Some of our previous subjects had died, other were on walkabout, but Granny Williams was still there.

She was now seventy-nine and bedridden. But she was as cheerful as ever, and as mentally alert. Again she was by far the best scorer. She guessed through the deck only 32 times in this series, but scored 76 more hits than were to be expected. The odds against this being a chance result are, once again, millions to one.

On this occasion, however, hers was not the only impressive evidence for the existence of E.S.P. Twelve subjects were tested. Six of these produced scores that, statistically, could not be attributed to chance.

Thus, in the first series, while Lizzie Williams contributed most of the extra-chance scoring leading to the over-all significance, on this occasion, probably due to our increased rapport with the natives, many more subjects presented evidence of E.S.P. Analysis of the secondary data, too, confirmed the primary.

The unequivocal claim may therefore be made that, under adequate test conditions, Australian aborigines have conclusively demonstrated extra-sensory perception. In general the last series would enable us to say that E.S.P. is probably more widespread among them than among whites.

Altogether, in our testing of E.S.P. among aborigines, Lyn and I recorded no less than 16,625 guesses. On the chance hypothesis about 3,325 of these should have been "hits," or correct guesses. In fact we recorded 3,870 hits. This was far beyond our best expectations, and far beyond the level necessary to establish the existence of the phenomenon.

E.S.P., however, was not the only side to this type of experimental work. Some evidence had been produced, particularly at Duke University, that a motor effect similar to E.S.P. existed. This was called psychokinesis, or P.K.—a sort of "mind-force." It was tested by having subjects "will" the fall of dice. Adequate precautions were taken against skilled manipulation of dice, dice bias (by having all faces as target an equal number of times), and the same stringent statistical criteria of significance were applied.

If this mind force were a fact, it could conceivably be employed by aboriginal doctors in, for example, making or breaking a storm, in the psychic killing of other natives, and so on.

We decided to carry the dice tests into the field also. At first we used small cubes with different colored faces instead of dice, but later switched to conventional, inlaid dice, supplied by Duke University, which we had our native subjects throw from a shaker lined with corrugated rubber.

The P.K. test provided rather more opportunities for friendly competition than the card test, and enthusiasm often ran high as natives competed against each other or for small rewards of tobacco and cigarettes.

But, despite many thousands of test runs, and occasional glimpses of what we thought at the time might be a P.K. effect, the final result, although better than chance expectation, did not reach the level of significance.

Although we felt that conditions were satisfactory for the demonstration of P.K. if it existed, perhaps they were not. These tests must be regarded as inconclusive.

An interesting sidelight of the P.K. tests in the desert areas was the natives' counting. No score was *eecha*, one was *nyinta*, two was *terra*. Three was obtained by combining one and two—*terra-min-nyinta*, and four was *terra-min-terra*. One or two of the brighter natives went as far as five with *terra-min-terra-min-nyinta* (two and two and one) but usually five or over was "big fellow mob."

We were successful in obtaining excellent evidence of E.S.P. Perhaps we were too impatient to get results in P.K.

The experimenter or observer who embarks on a study of the aborigines, and particularly of aboriginal magic, must be patient. Aborigines are extremely reticent. They will not perpetuate their secrets in their own young people whom they do not consider worthy. They would rather let the secrets perish. It is not surprising that they sometimes avoid or evade the white man's curiosity or, at a less conscious level, do not give themselves freely to his tests.

The field is a difficult one but, if the obstacles can be overcome, it is a field that can produce riches of many kinds.

Some of these riches may seem mere statistics. But, in our investigations, these statistics, by their degree of relative precision and freedom from opinion, gave aboriginal magic a less ephemeral character than it had had before.

Unfortunately, the field testing, the first of its kind with native peoples in any part of the world, was time consuming and, up to a point, cumbersome. Future experimenters in this field should be able, after scrutiny of the existing material, both anecdotal and experimental, and a review of new methods that might be devised and existing methods that might be modified, to adopt a procedure that will simplify the techniques in this field.

They should be able to embark on a program with the knowledge that, however inadequate the map may be in its details, the main features of aboriginal magic have been marked, and the possible sources of error greatly reduced.

CHAPTER 17

Problems Solved

In the morning Tjalkalieri and I took our customary stroll to the sand hills. I had nothing specific to discuss with him. Idly we watched the activities of the natives about the camp in the distance; we contemplated the scurrying ants weaving fantastic patterns of tracks in the smooth sand between the clumps of spinifex, and Tjalkalieri traced with his finger a *corroboree* pattern that was similar in design.

We were both sad, for the time to part was fast approaching. For us it was to be a final parting—he had no address and he could not read even if I did write and a letter reached him.

"Tjalkalieri," I said, "all this magic, your clever-men able to kill people, making people better, bringing rain, and doing other great things, all this means a good deal to you."

"It is good for us," he said. Then, after a moment of silence he repeated, "It is good for us. It is the way we live. It is different from the white man, but it is good for us."

I was conscious that language had been a constant barrier between us. If it could have been reduced further or removed, he might have got across to me some of his profounder thoughts on the meaning and importance of magic. It was remarkable he had been able to convey what he had.

I believe on this occasion he was trying to say, "These

230

beliefs about magic are not fantastic to us. The cures that our doctors make are real, practical and important. Magic disciplines our lives. We give to it and receive from it. Our beliefs about magic are valid for us."

I was, of course, interested in whether or not aboriginal magic had an independent validity as well. Tjalkalieri had seemed to stress its social significance. And he was right, for, quite independently of the reality of some of the phenomena that comprise it, magic has a good deal to validate and justify it.

It impinges on every aspect of aboriginal belief and activity, from the magico-religious mythology to hunting and sexual favor. Even if it were entirely superstitious, which it obviously is not, it is vigorous, subtle, comprehensive. It guides the native in his activities, it provides a framework of conventional behavior, it prescribes the penalties for infringement, and provides the means for enforcing them. It is an active and vital force, an instrument of the will, and a protection from the will of others.

Magic is the means by which co-operative activities may be enforced and activities inimical to tribal welfare suppressed. To a very great extent the power rests with the elders of a group who, appropriately directing magical decisions and the behavior of the tribal clever-men, adopt it as a channel for political influence.

An aspect of magic that appears to have received little attention is that in many of its applications it reduces wasteful physical conflict by diverting violent emotions into legitimate and physically less damaging channels. It enables the native to express, albeit in a modified way, many of the emotions and desires that modern civilization requires we should suppress in ourselves. This we may presume to be of some benefit to the individual, and probably also to the ultimate good of the community.

Magic is thus a unifying influence in aboriginal society.

What, however, of the facts underlying magic?

Lyn and I had established that E.S.P. occurred among aborigines. This being so, the instances in which natives displayed a knowledge of distant events and circumstances, as in the multitude of crisis cases we recorded, became explicable.

In the experimental work with white people tests have been diverse and involved, correlation with personality factors has been established, refinement of techniques has led to more and more detailed knowledge of E.S.P. And, as the research has advanced to further stages of inquiry, one thing has become very clear: the processes involved in E.S.P. have the same essence of normality as less uncommon mental phenomena.

As with white people, so also with the aborigines—there is really no question of the supernatural. The phenomenon of telepathy is rare, it usually occurs in heavily charged emotional circumstances, as at the time of a person's death or illness, but it is a mode of communication that, though relatively uncommon, and often unreliable and incomplete, appears to be universal.

Research with the aborigines made some contribution to parapsychology also, for it showed that mediation of information in a dramatic way—by a vision or apparition in the case of whites and some detribalized natives, but by the totem in the case of less sophisticated aborigines—was essentially conditioned by the social background and belief of the person involved.

The positive results in the E.S.P. work also explained the instances where telepathy presumably occurs in conjunction with smoke signals, in cases where a problem is specifically put to the dream state, and in instances where clever-men apparently travel in a self-induced trance and acquire information. It may occur in some cases of love magic.

Here again a useful contribution was made to general research in parapsychology, for it is in these circumstances that, apparently, the aboriginal doctor can exercise E.S.P. at a conscious level. And it is this conscious control of the process that has been so elusive in research among whites. With an understanding of the outlook and attitude of the aboriginal doctor, a better understanding of the process becomes available. And all aborigines have an outlook of anticipation and belief and expectation that the unusual will occur—and a ready, uncritical acceptance of it when it does.

We established that aborigines are extremely suggestible, that they respond to hypnotic influence very readily, and that, taking advantage of their prestige, aboriginal doctors in fact practice hypnotism to achieve a variety of effects.

Suggestion is a force which, in our society, we use to some effect in a rather modified way—in advertising and propaganda, for example, and in some aspects of psychosomatic medicine. It is, however, an integral part of, and necessary to, the aboriginal way of life. And here its effects are far more startling.

It is at the core of all the aboriginal doctors' cures, for it links with the native mythology, the prestige of the doctor, priest of the Dream Time, and becomes an active force. It links, too, with a symbolism, as in the removal of magical objects from an ailing person's body, so that the symbolism becomes reality—and the results astound us. The effective use of suggestion by the native doctors, reinforced with trickery and sleight of hand, is a remarkable achievement.

Suggestion is the key, also, to the bone-pointing events and other magical killings. It is a far more potent force with aborigines than with us. An interesting aspect of bone pointing is that the probable growth of the practice was from the discovery that a person scratched with a bone from a putrefying animal often became ill and died. Eventually the mere pointing of a bone became sufficient in itself.

Potent though suggestion is, its most advanced form in hypnotism has been developed by aborigines, so that all the wide range of phenomena that can be produced by this means we know now to be available to aboriginal doctors. That they practice it in one form, using the magical quartz crystals, so similar to western practice, is a remarkable coincidence. Doctors gaze into crystals themselves to induce slight hypnotic trance states and then present their prophecies and prognostications.

With hypnotism native clever-men can effect cures, and produce hallucinations and illusions. This, in conjunction with trickery such as spittle-manipulation and the *Gordius* hairworm, is almost certainly the explanation of the fabulous stories of the aboriginal doctors' magic cords. Posthypnotic suggestion, associated with skillful opportunism, is probably the explanation of stories of fast travel.

In all of these subtle practices there is evidence that the aboriginal clever-man is well aware of underlying psychological principles. We must see him, then, not as a charlatan, but as a skilled practitioner in an extraordinarily difficult field.

Our tests with P.K. failed to indicate that aborigines could exercise any direct "mind-over-matter" force. The making of storms, and other aspects where a direct magical influence on nature would seem to be indicated, probably can be explained by the doctors' superior knowledge of the subtle signs of nature and resultant timing of his own activities.

Doctors claim to have brought storms by magical means but often, it is likely, their claims are made after the event. The accounts we recorded of this and other phenomena were probably all distorted in some way, molded to fit the conventional pattern, first in the observation itself, and later again in the recounting of the incident.

In aboriginal magic there is trickery and deception, malobservation, exaggeration, and distortion; there is confusion between cause and effect; there is a mixture of apparently genuine psychical manifestations with religious beliefs and superstitions; there is credulity imposed on by cunning—all

occurring against a background of belief (as in the aborigines'
strange, living mythology) and modes of thinking that are
widely different from our own.

But aboriginal magic has its reality, for E.S.P. is real, the
powers of suggestion and hypnotism are real, and the results
achieved by a wide variety of tricks and devices are real.

Aboriginal magic is, so to speak, laid bare—but it is not to
be despised; for in it we find practitioners achieving results in
mental phenomena that have puzzled us for some time, exercising a subtle art with confidence and skill, in many ways a
model for our future investigations into some of man's strange
powers.

A multitude of questions still arise, mostly now on minor
points. We must answer them while we can. But we cannot
afford to dally. Masses of data lie embedded in rocks for
geologists to pick over at their leisure; chemists, physicists,
even psychologists, have material at hand for all time. The
parapsychologist who concerns himself with native peoples
like the aborigines becomes keenly aware, as he sees elderly
natives die and sophistication proceed, that valuable material
is slipping all too rapidly away from him.

Whatever work is to be done with the aborigines must be
done soon. The aboriginal population is not diminishing so
rapidly that we can yet see its end, but the process of acculturation is going on at an alarming rate, and it cannot be
long before "untouched" groups will be found only in the most
remote parts of the country.

In the afternoon the truck was loaded. Lyn and I put our
gear on board and took our final look around the Hermannsburg Mission.

Soon all was ready and the pastors, the headstockman, the
other whites living their isolated lives in this remote outpost
of their church, gathered with their wives and children around
the truck.

We made our farewells, and Stanley started the engine. Then I noticed a native in the background, standing respectfully at a distance. He was smiling, but there were tears in his eyes. He had taken off his battered felt hat and was crushing it self-consciously between his hands.

I walked across to him and held out my hand.

"Good-by, Tjalkalieri," I said.

He was silent for a moment.

"Good-by," he answered. Then he permitted himself an intimacy he had not dared before.

"Good-by, my friend——my good friend."

I climbed on board. Stanley revved the motor and we pulled slowly out of the compound onto the rough track.

We looked back. The group of waving people was obscured by dust and rapidly growing smaller as the truck picked up speed.

A short distance from them stood a solitary, lonely man. . . .

APPENDIX A

For the statistically minded the following table sets out, in highly digested form, the results of the four series of tests carried out with aboriginal subjects.

In the case of E.S.P. a "Run" consists of the calling through once of the deck of 25 cards, in P.K. a "Run" is 24 single dice throws regardless of the number of dice thrown at one time.

The "Deviation" is the difference of the actual score from the chance expectation. "CR" stands for "Critical Ratio" and is a statistical measure of significance.

E.S.P. Tests

Location	Runs	Hits	Dev.	Av. Score	C.R.
Woodenbong (1st series)	296	1,706	+226	5.76	6.57
Tabulam	59	319	+ 24	5.41	1.56
Central Australia	171	907	+ 52	5.30	1.99
Woodenbong (2nd series)	139	938	+243	6.75	10.31
Totals	665	3,870	+545	5.82	10.57

P.K. Tests

Location	Runs	Hits	Dev.	Av. Score	C.R.
Woodenbong (1st series)	1,896	7,712	+128	4.07	1.61
Tabulam	168	645	− 27	3.84	1.14
Central Australia	1,128	4,519	+ 7	4.01	0.11
Woodenbong (2nd series)	312	1,254	+ 6	4.01	0.19
Totals	3,504	14,130	+114	4.03	1.1

APPENDIX B

It is not possible to give in full the details of all of the tests applied
to the aborigines, but it is thought that the following Questionnaire,
which gave rise to a good many of the anecdotal accounts, will be
of interest. The wording of questions was varied as circumstances
demanded. Some questions were intended to test the *belief* of subjects. These are marked with an asterisk.*

Questionnaire

Name.........   Location...........   Caste............

Age......   Tribal Group.......   Literacy..........

*1. Would you know if a relative some distance away died, had
an accident, or was seriously ill? (How?)

2. Has this ever happened to you?
   (Details: i. When?
             ii. Full circumstances.
            iii. Accuracy of information.
             iv. Mediating vehicle.)

3. Have you ever had an experience (feeling) of this sort and
later found you were wrong?

4. Have you ever seen the spirit of someone who was dead?
   (Details: i. Did you know the person was dead at the time?
             ii. Relationship?
            iii. Distance involved?
             iv. Times.
              v. Accuracy of information.)

*5. Do you think that when you die your spirit will continue to live?

(Details: i. How long?
         ii. Communicate with living?
         iii. Spirits of other people survive?)

6. Have you ever seen (or heard, etc.) a spirit that was not a dead person's spirit—e.g., "little red man"? (Poltergeists?)

7. (a) Have you heard of smoke signals being made to send messages?

   (b) Was the message in the smoke itself, i.e., was the smoke like writing? Or was the smoke a sign for a clever-man (or someone else) to be ready for a message?

8. I have heard that clever-men could tell what was happening a long way away at the same time as it was happening—

  *(a) Do you think this is possible?

  (b) Do you know of this happening? (Details)

  (c) Do you know of anyone other than a clever-man who could do this?

9. I have heard that some clever-men could tell things before they happened, say what would happen tomorrow or the next day—

  *(a) Do you think this is possible?

  (b) Have you heard of this happening? (Details)

  (c) Do you know of anyone who was not clever who could do this?

10. Have you ever seen a clever-man make another person go to sleep?

(Details: i. How did he do this?
         ii. What else happened?)

11. (a) Do you know of dreams ever telling of, say, the death or sickness of a relative some distance away, or something the person could not have known otherwise? (Details)

  (b) Would such dreams be different in any way from ordinary dreams? How?

(c) Do you know of a clever-man telling other people what their dreams mean?

12. I have heard that clever-men can talk to the dead—
  * (a) Do you think this is possible?
  (b) Do you know of this happening? (Details)
  (c) Does the dead person answer? (How?)

13. Some clever-men say they have spirit dogs or spirit snakes that help them—
  * (a) Do you think this is true?
  (b) Have you ever seen any of these spirit animals?

14. (a) Have you ever seen a clever-man cure someone who was sick or who had had an accident?
  (b) What did he do?
  (c) Did the sick person get well?

15. I have heard that some clever-men could make rain or call up a storm. They said they could also stop storms—
  * (a) Do you think this is possible?
  (b) Have you ever seen this happen? (Details)

16. I have heard that some clever-men could fly to the top of a tree or climb there by a rope they made come out of themselves—
  * (a) Do you think this is possible?
  (b) Have you ever seen anything like this? (Details)

17. I have heard that some clever-men could make themselves invisible, just disappear when there was nowhere they could hide—
  * (a) Do you think this is possible?
  (b) Have you ever heard of this happening? (Details)
  (c) Have you had any personal experience of this? (Details)

18. Some clever-men say they can travel long distances very quickly, faster than a car (Distinguish between spirit and actual)—
  * (a) Do you think this is true?
  (b) Have you ever heard of this happening? (Details)
  (c) Have you had any personal experience of this? (Details)

240